JOHN
SINGER
SARGENT

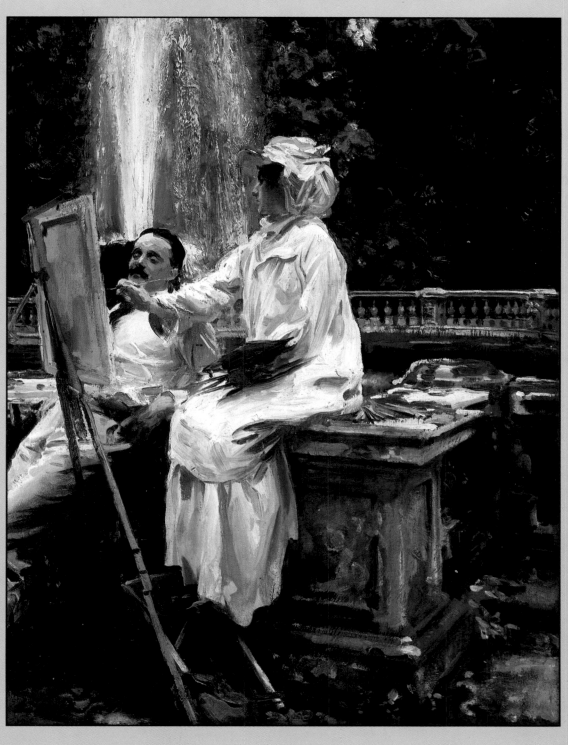

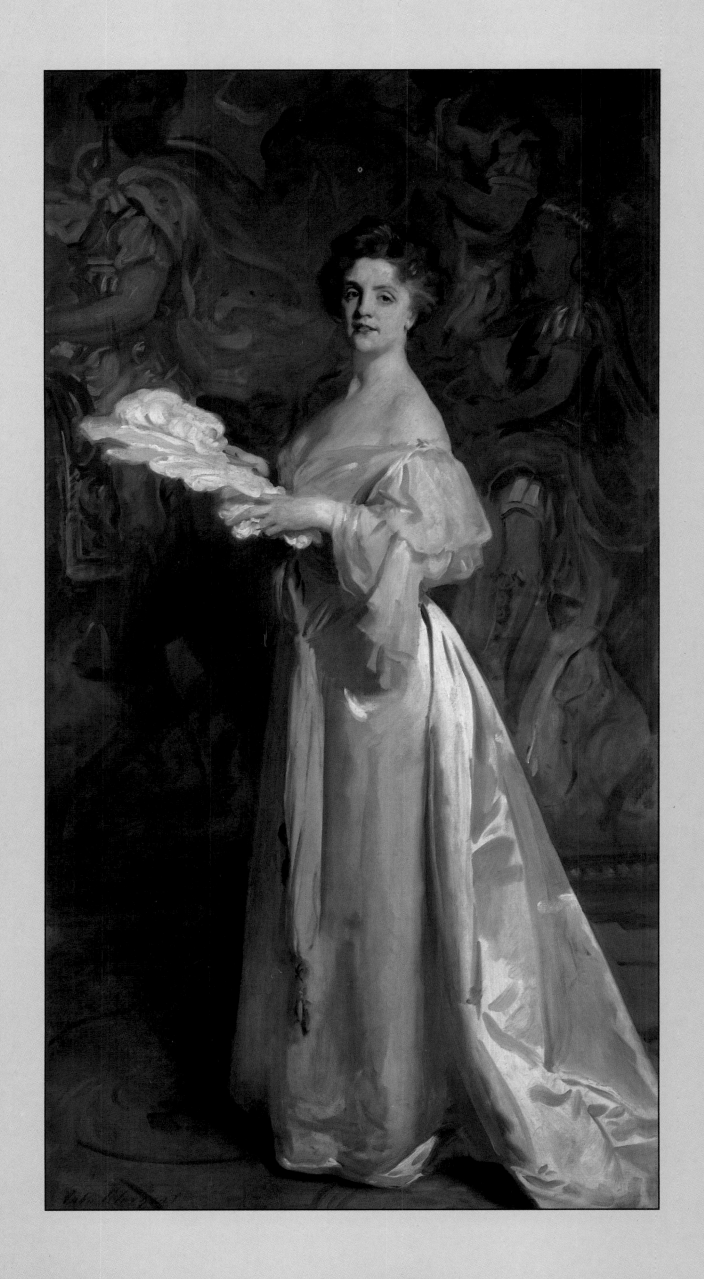

John Singer Sargent

Kate F. Jennings

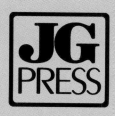

JG PRESS

Page 1:
The Fountain, Villa Torlonia, Frascati
1907, oil on canvas, 28½×22 in.
Friends of American Art Collection,
The Art Institute of Chicago
(1914.57)

Page 2:
Ada Rehan
1894-95, oil on canvas, 93×50⅛ in.
Bequest of Catharine Lasell Whitlin, 1940,
in memory of Ada Rehan,
The Metropolitan Museum of Art, New York, NY
(40.146)

These pages:
Breakfast in the Loggia
1910, oil on canvas, 20½×28 in.
Freer Gallery of Art,
Smithsonian Institution, Washington, DC

Reprinted 2004 by
World Publications Group, Inc.
455 Somerset Avenue
North Dighton, MA 02764
www.wrldpub.com

ISBN 1-57215-341-5

Printed and bound in China by
Leefung-Asco Printers Trading Ltd.

8 7 6 5

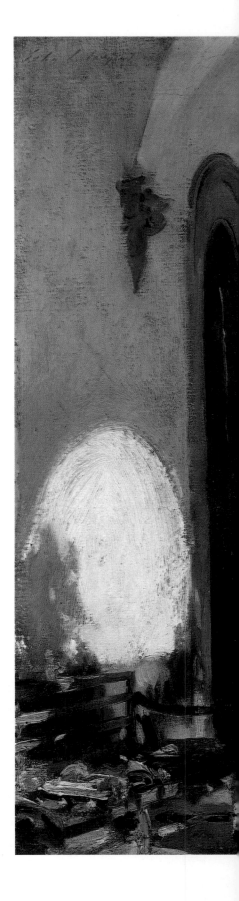

Contents

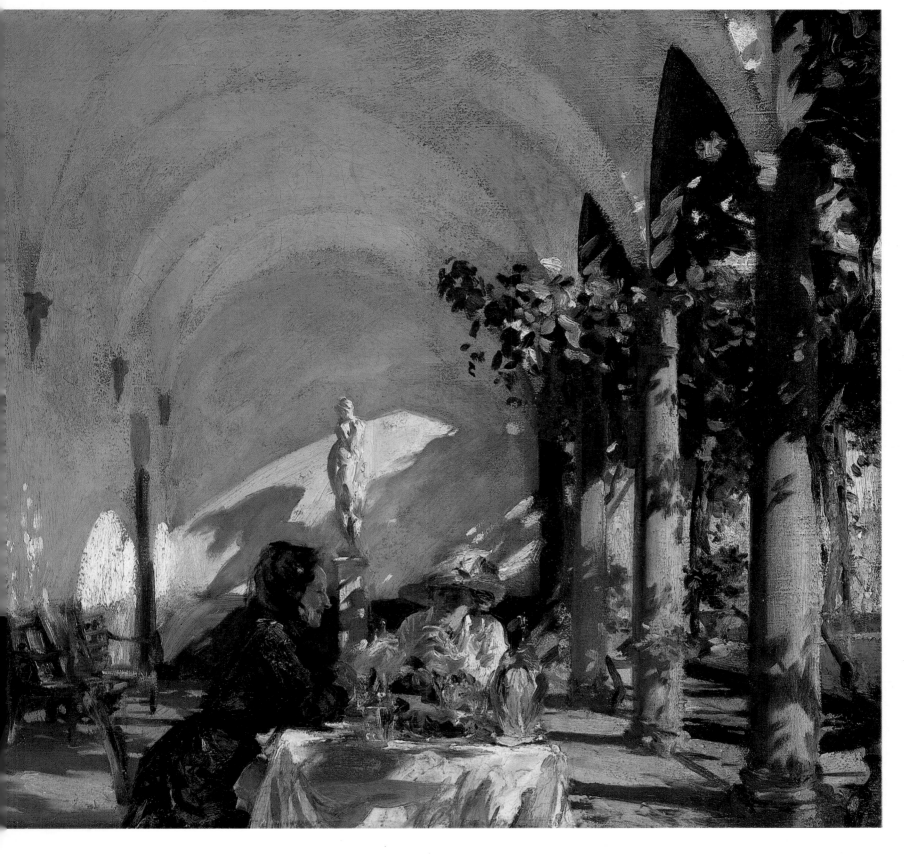

5

INTRODUCTION

John Singer Sargent was born on January 12, 1856 in Florence, Italy to expatriate American parents who travelled abroad in search of European refinement and elegance. Sargent's talent would synthesize the classical and romantic virtues of his European education with the directness and vigor of his native heritage. The result would be a remarkable, enduring legacy of portraits, landscape paintings, and public murals that continue to inspire artists, writers, and viewers today.

John Singer Sargent's father, Dr. Fitzwilliam Sargent, was a surgeon who had retired from a lucrative practice in Philadelphia, Pennsylvania. Dr. Sargent had also illustrated several medical textbooks. John's mother, Mary Newbold Singer Sargent, yearned to attain the cachet and cultivation that exposure to the arts on the continent could avail to her family. Mary was an accomplished amateur watercolorist and enjoyed playing the piano, two avocations she would instill in her son at a young age.

As a result of Mary Sargent's restless, questing nature, once

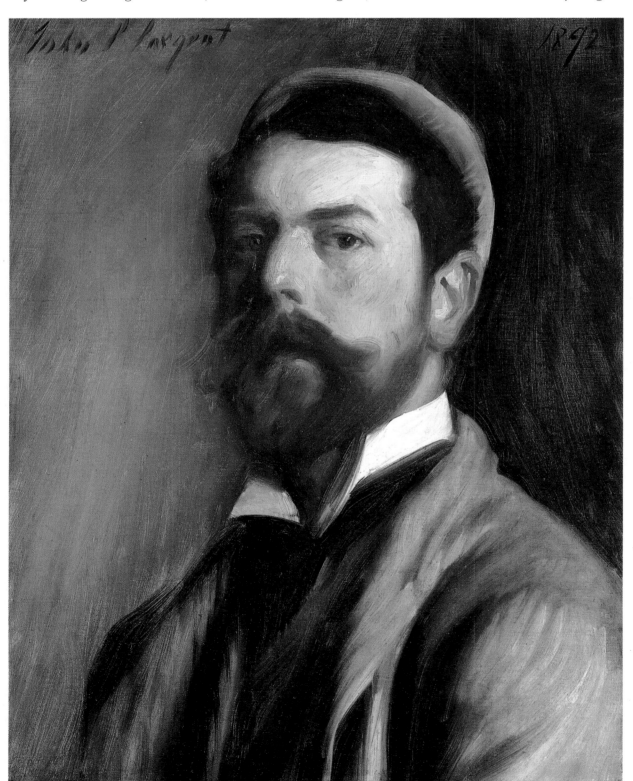

Left: John Singer Sargent painted this self-portrait in 1892 when he was 36.

Right above: The painter who probably influenced Sargent most (and to whom he is most often compared) was the seventeenth-century Spanish artist Diego Velázquez, whose "Mujer" is shown here.

Right: Sargent's 1889 study "My Dining Room."

6

in Europe the family rarely stayed in any one place for long. They lived in Nice, Paris, London, Rome, and parts of Germany and toured other cities frequently over the course of John Sargent's childhood. His artistic skill was precocious and he made excellent use of these sightseeing forays. A passage from one of his letters to a friend, Ben Castillo, at the age of nine, reflects his early disposition to draw:

> We spent several weeks in London, and the things which interested me most there were the Zoological Gardens, the Crystal Palace, the South Kensington Museum. At the Zoological Gardens we saw the lions fed, and I rode on a camel's neck, and Emily and I rode on an elephant. I made several drawings of the animals there. At the Crystal Palace we saw models of some of the animals which lived upon the earth before man. I copied several of them: the Iguanodon, Labryinthodon, Pterodactyle, Ickthyosaurus, Megalosaurus and Mammoth.
>
> At the South Kensington Museum we saw some very fine paintings of Landseer, the celebrated animal painter, and a very fine picture by Rosa Bonheur called the horse fair, but the most curious thing there was an oyster forming a pearl; the oyster was in spirits of wine.

John Sargent's constant companion throughout his youth and fellow traveller and soulmate during his later years was his sister, Emily. She was a year younger than her brother. The deaths in childhood of both an older and a younger sister accentuated the bond between John and Emily. Violet Sargent was born fourteen years after John and would later marry Francis Ormond.

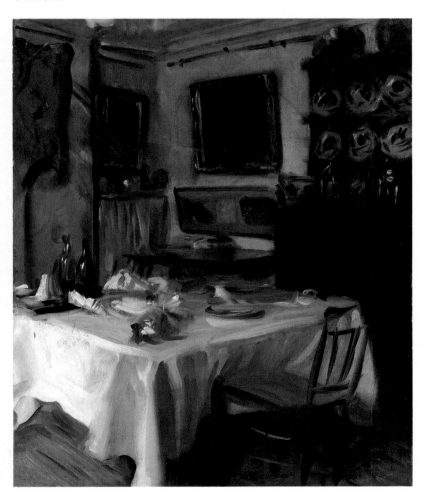

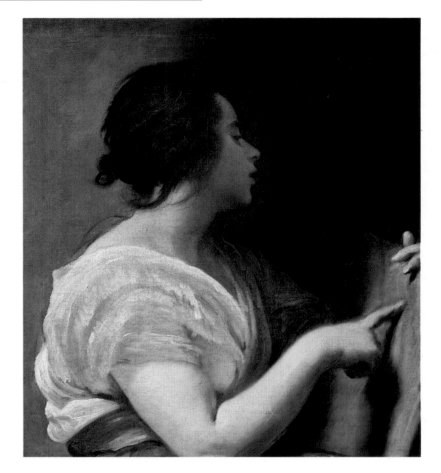

Recognizing their son's talent, Mary and Fitzwilliam enrolled John Singer Sargent at the Academia di Belle Arti in Florence when he was fourteen. The Sargents were part of a community there of British and American artists and writers. The wife of a diplomat who met Sargent at this time had this impression of the young artist: "A big-eyed, sentimental, charming boy, playing the mandolin very pleasantly." Music was an integral part of the family's life and many evenings were spent at concerts or giving recitals at home.

Sargent quickly grew bored with the routine of the academy. When it closed one winter for three months or when he had a sprained ankle that kept him at home, his spirit and ambition were ever buoyant: ". . . I have a very handsome Neapolitan model to draw and paint, who plays on the Zampogna and tamburino and dances tarantellas for us when he is tired of sitting.'

Sargent's family continued their travels and excursions to Dresden, Germany, to Switzerland and the Tyrol. John Sargent had the occasion in Venice to meet the most famous American artist abroad, James Abbott McNeill Whistler, a noted portraitist and one whose talents would later be eclipsed by Sargent. In Venice, Sargent also saw the art of the Renaissance painters and wrote to his cousin, "I have learned in Venice to admire Tintoretto immensely and to consider him perhaps second only to Michelangelo and Titian, whose beauties it was his aim to unite."

In August of 1874, the Sargents settled in Paris and John entered the École des Beaux Arts. By October, at the age of eighteen, Sargent was taking studio classes with Carolus Duran, a popular Parisian portraitist of Spanish origin. Duran espoused the virtues of his fellow Spaniard, the seventeenth-century painter Diego Velázquez, almost to the exclusion of other artists.

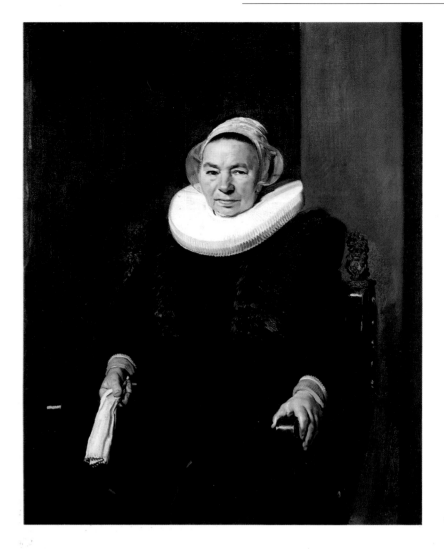

Duran also emphasized simplified schemes and the importance of color values and halftones. Sargent's abilities and patronage would soon supersede those of his master yet he retained a lifelong respect for Carolus Duran's teaching skills and he acknowledged his debt to this artist's style. Later in life, while reviewing a painting by a younger student, Sargent remarked: "That has value. I wonder who taught him to do that. I thought Carolus was the only man who taught that. He couldn't do it himself, but he could teach it."

At the École des Beaux Arts, J. Alden Weir, the American Impressionist, was a fellow student of Sargent's, and Auguste Rodin, the sculptor, was a friend of the young artist. The late 1870s was a fertile time for an artist to be in Paris and Sargent was exposed to a variety of schools and techniques. Among these were the Barbizon group of romantic landscape painters, the exquisite draftsman Ingres, and Courbet and the Realists. The Salon des Refusés, including Manet, Degas, and the Impressionists was another influence.

In 1876, at the age of twenty, Sargent made his first visit to the United States. He returned in the fall of the same year to Paris and in 1878 was commissioned, along with his teacher, Duran, to paint portraits of one another for a ceiling in the Louvre. In the Salon of 1878 Sargent won honorable mention for his painting "En Route Pour la Pĕche" and during the summer of 1878 he worked at a monastery in Capri. There he painted Rosina, a young woman he described as "an AnaCapri girl, a magnificent type."

Two years later Sargent was in Morocco staying at the Hotel Central Tangier, where he worked on sketches of Moorish buildings. In Morocco the excitement of gypsy dances captured his attention. Sargent began a series of sketches in preparation for one of his early masterpieces "El Jaleo," a splendid, lively canvas full of the vivacity of Spanish music and the brio of Spanish dancing.

In Holland, Sargent studied Frans Hals. Hals and Velázquez were the primary influences upon Sargent in the realm of portrait painting. This is shown by his remarks to a younger friend who had written to him for advice: "Begin with Frans Hals, copy and study Frans Hals, after that go to Madrid and copy Velázquez, leave Velázquez till you have got all you can out of Frans Hals." It sounds like a relentless and circuitous route but these two artists were guiding lights for Sargent.

During the 1880s Sargent began to receive the patronage and critical success that artists strive for but seldom find. He had many portrait commissions in Paris and a full-length portrait brought him 8000 francs, a half-length portrait, 5000 francs.

Society matrons and wealthy, prominent citizens all desired to be painted by Sargent, and though he accommodated their wishes, he was not entirely content to accede to their demands. However, the portraits flourished and they are wonderful records of the era when he lived.

Sargent won the second place medal from the Salon in Paris in 1881 and received accolades for his Salon pictures of 1882, among these "Mrs. Austin" and "El Jaleo." Jules Comte, an art reviewer for *L'Illustration*, proclaimed, "one does not know which to admire most, the simplicity of the means which the artist has employed or the brilliance of the result which he has achieved."

From Paris, Sargent travelled often to Venice, Rome, and Siena. In 1883 he saw a woman he desired to paint named Madame Gautreau and enlisted the aid of a friend to secure the role of her portraitist.

He wrote: "I have a great desire to paint her portrait and have reason to think she would allow it and is waiting for someone to propose this homage to her beauty. If you are bien avec elle and will see her in Paris you might tell her I am a man of prodigious talent."

However, actually to do the painting was not as wonderful as the artist had anticipated. He sent a letter to a close friend, Vernon Lee, describing the work in progress: "Your letter has just reached me . . . struggling with the unpaintable beauty and hopeless laziness of Madame Gautreau."

The work was not well received and was openly criticized at the Salon of 1884, especially the décolletage of Madame Gautreau's dress. By today's standards she looks suitably attired for an evening in Paris and quite alluring. Sargent sold the painting to the Metropolitan Museum of Art in New York in 1916, and wrote the following letter to Edward Robinson, then Director of the Metropolitan:

My dear Ned,

. . . My portrait of Mme. Gautreau is now with some other things I sent from here at the San Francisco exhibition and now that it is in America I

Far left: "Mevrouw Bodolphe" by Frans Hals, another painter who much influenced Sargent.

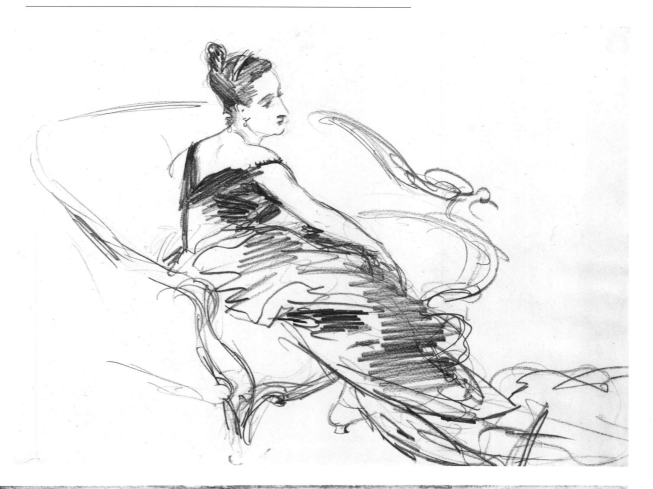

Right: One of Sargent's preliminary studies for "Madame X."

Below: Another preliminary study by Sargent, this one for "El Jaleo."

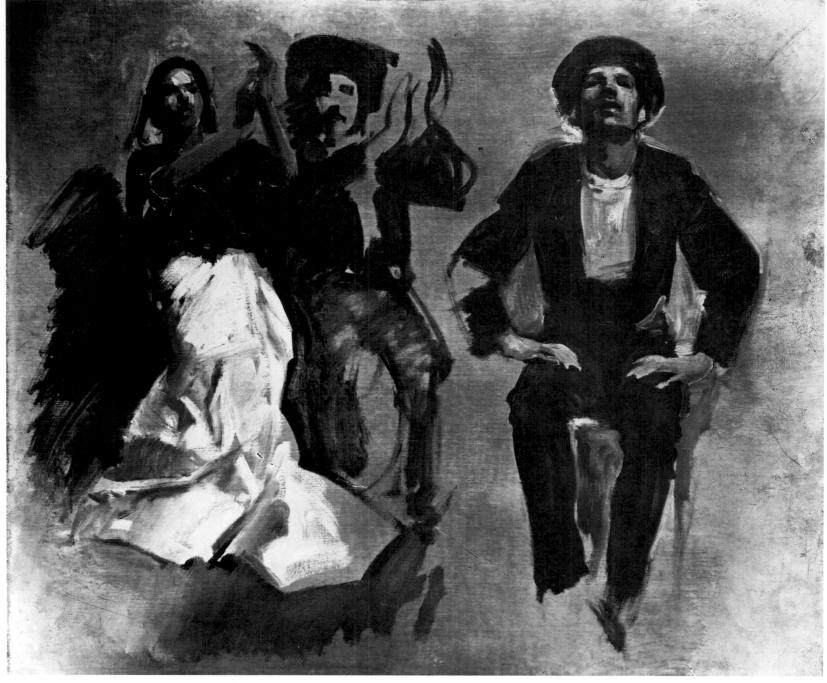

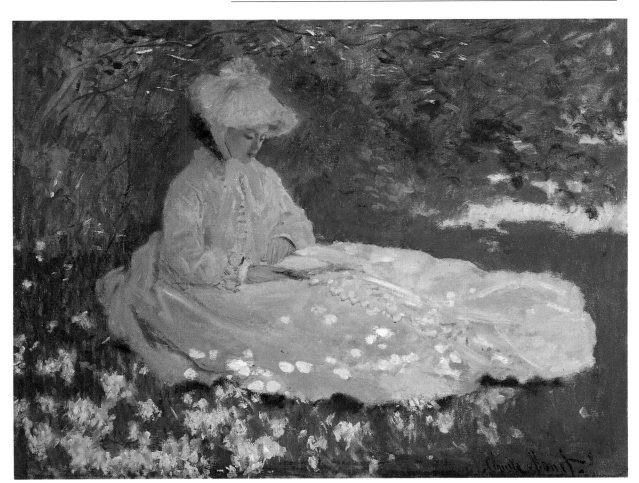

Left: Claude Monet's 1875 "A Woman in a Garden, Springtime." Sargent never joined the Impressionist movement but nevertheless admired many painters in the group, notably Monet.

Right: A dim photograph, taken in 1886 in Broadway, England, of Sargent at his easel.

Far right: A photograph of Sargent taken in Worcester, Massachusetts.

rather feel inclined to let it stay there if a Museum should want it. I suppose it is the best thing I have done. I would let the Metropolitan Museum have it for £1000 . . . Let me know your opinion . . .

However, when he was in his late twenties, the scandal caused by this the portrait was difficult for Sargent and added to the ennui he had begun to feel in Paris. He yearned for new environs: "I am dreadfully tired of the people here and of my present work, a certain majestic portrait of an ugly woman. She is like a great frigate under full sail with homeward-bound streamers."

In the winter of 1885 Sargent moved from Paris to London where the social climate and the artistic community welcomed his arrival. The portraits of this era, the late 1880s to early 1900s, are of many of Sargent's literary friends including Henry James and Robert Louis Stevenson. Stevenson recorded this impression of his picture: "Sargent has been and painted my portrait: a very nice fellow he is, and is supposed to have done well; it is a poetical but very chicken-boned figurehead, as thus represented." This particular portrait is an unusual rendering of the writer pacing while his wife lounges on a wicker chair, wearing a Spanish shawl. It is atypical of Sargent's portraiture yet an incisive, apt character study.

Sargent painted his contemporaries in the art world as well – Ralph Curtis, William Merritt Chase, Paul Helleu, and Claude Monet are notable among these. During this time he visited Monet at Giverny in France. In England, during his summer vacations in the late 1880s, Sargent went to Broadway, a Cotswold village and resort colony outside London. Here he worked side by side with other painters and writers and his paintings from this time have a definite Impressionist style.

While at Broadway, Sargent often went to regattas and sporting events on the Avon and the Thames. He made several oil sketches and free-spirited portraits of his friends engaged in boating parties and resting and fishing by the riverside.

At Broadway Sargent lived with the Millets and his artist friend, Edwin Abbey, at Farnham House. Henry James was there also. In London during the autumn and winter social seasons, Sargent lived in a studio apartment at 13 Tite Street. Here Sargent painted the portraits of many young society ladies and grande dames in the fashionable, privileged circles.

When Sargent had visited London from Paris, among his first English patrons were the Vickers. Mrs. Albert Vickers was featured in his painting "Dinner Table at Night" of 1884 and her son and daughter were the models in the 1884 painting "Children in a Garden." The Vickers's cousins, the daughters of Colonel Thomas V. Vickers, were the young ladies in Sargent's first group portrait "The Misses Vickers."

Other ladies in the London social whirl such as Mrs. George Winton, Mrs. Henry White, Miss Helen Sears, and the Wyndham Sisters figured in this series of paintings. These portraits had their liabilities for Sargent. He described one of a Mrs. Hammersley with these words, "I have begun the routine of painting with anxious relatives hanging on my brush. Mrs. H. has a mother."

In Sargent's 1903 portrait of Mrs. Fiske Warren and her daughter, Rachel, both wear simple flowing pink gowns that set off their brunette hair. The deep brown background allows them to project forward in the picture plane and touches of light from golden statuettes of winged seraphim add to a sense of luxury and delicate femininity. The two ladies have "Mona Lisa" smiles.

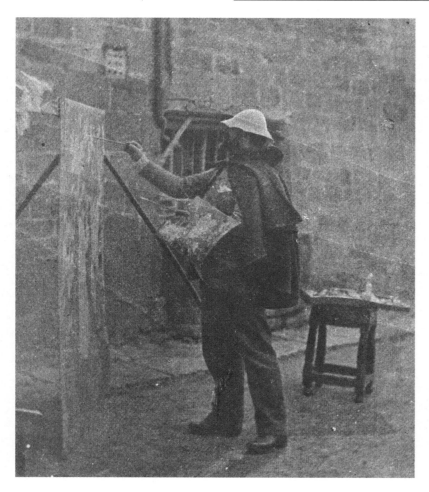
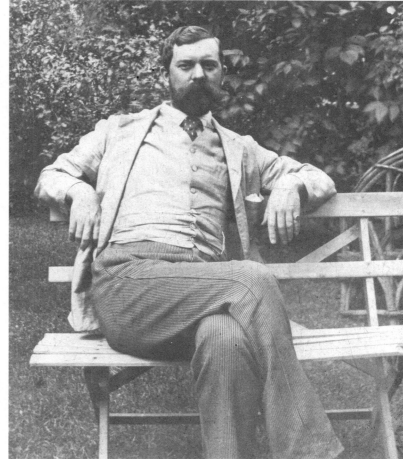

One of the sadder moments in the artist's life was the death of his father, Dr. Fitzwilliam Sargent, in April of 1889. He had been an invalid for quite some time and Sargent had been very attentive. Dr. Sargent had accompanied his wife to Europe and encouraged his son's interests in music, art, and literature. He was more retiring than she and was wistful for America on several occasions, as well as the prospect of a more permanent place to raise his family. His son would later fulfill some of his father's dreams when he returned to Boston and his Sargent roots to furnish murals and canvases for the public library and museum of art there.

An art student, Miss J. H. Heyneman, had this impression of Sargent when she met him during the 1890s: "In any company he seemed to tower over every one else in the room, as much by reason of his personality as through the accident of his height . . . his close-cut beard was dark brown and his thick hair and sharply marked eyebrows were almost black. On his broad shoulders his head looked small, and was chiefly remarkable for the beauty of the brow, which was splendidly broad and full." He was physically imposing, at six feet tall and carried considerable weight over his frame.

Sargent was elected an Associate of the Royal Academy in 1894. In 1897 he was elected a full Royal Academician. He taught at the Royal Academy schools and his words of advice to young student friends reflect his own techniques and style: "You can't do sketches enough. Sketch everything and keep your curiosity fresh." When an ambitious young artist wrote for advice about becoming a portrait painter, Sargent replied, "Become a painter first and then apply your knowledge to a special branch – but do not begin with what is required for a special branch or you will become a mannerist."

Sargent also felt it was important to capture a likeness readily, on a first go at the canvas if possible. He might work for weeks along one tack but if he felt it was wrong he would discard it, begin anew, and finish the portrait in three sittings. He would do sixteen canvases if necessary to get it right and fresh rather than rework a marred study. Sargent's clients were no less exhausted than he on occasion and they were aware he might reveal more of their characters thean they wished. As one remarked afterwards, "It's positively dangerous to sit for Sargent. It's taking your face in your hands." One woman disliked Sargent's rendering of her nose and he countered with "Oh, you can alter a little thing like that when you get it home."

Sargent's bold, physical approach to painting was unusual. He would shout "Demons," rush at the canvas, place a flurry of brush strokes and then retreat to a distance to find out what effect his marks had from this perspective. The easel was set up next to the person being portrayed but he viewed it from afar.

Sargent felt that a rapport between the artist and sitter was very important and had the insight into the nature of portrait painting that "Women don't ask you to make them beautiful but you can feel them wanting you to do so all the time." Music was an integral part of the painting process for Sargent. Once when he was stymied with a particular lady's portrait, he asked her husband to play a duet with him on the piano – it seemed to solve whatever difficulty had arisen and he completed the canvas soon after.

Music by Wagner, Strauss, Debussy, and Spanish composers appealed to Sargent and he was so gifted a pianist that musician C.M. Loeffler wrote "had he chosen to become a musician, he would have risen to eminence in our art in one way or another." This was confirmed by another musician, Percy Grainger, "to hear Sargent play the piano was indeed a treat."

In 1891 Sargent's youngest sister, Violet, had married Francis Ormond and she and her two daughters, Reine and Rose-Marie were the subjects of many sketches and paintings. Sargent often travelled with the Ormonds in addition to his mother and sister Emily.

Sargent had a studio in New York City in the 1890s and painted several notable Americans at this atelier on 23rd Street. Among these were Senator Henry Cabot Lodge, Katherine Pratt, and Edwin Booth. He also painted a Spanish dancer named "Carmencita" whom he had to bribe to model for him.

One of Sargent's important patrons in London was Asher Wertheimer, a prominent and successful art dealer whose portrait Sargent painted in 1898. In his pencil sketch of Wertheimer, the dealer's form is quickly and simply contoured, his

Chesterfield coat is suggested with a few dark strokes about the collar and lapels. His steady head carriage and authoritative gaze are indicated with a minimum of detail. His head appears quite small in relationship to his imposing stature.

In the finished oil painting, Wertheimer's expression is more contented, as if he were pleased with a good sale. His bearing is proud yet a covetous and acquisitive nature is also conveyed – his eyes are beady and he has the piercing, almost intimidating look of one accustomed to appraisals. With a cigar in hand, wearing a starched, white collar and with a gold watch chain across his vest, he is a picture of wealth and worldly success, the master of his destiny. Wertheimer had Sargent paint his wife at the same time in honor of their twenty-fifth wedding anniversary. Sargent portrayed Wertheimer's daughters, Ena and Betty, in 1901, standing next to one another in white satin and red velvet gowns.

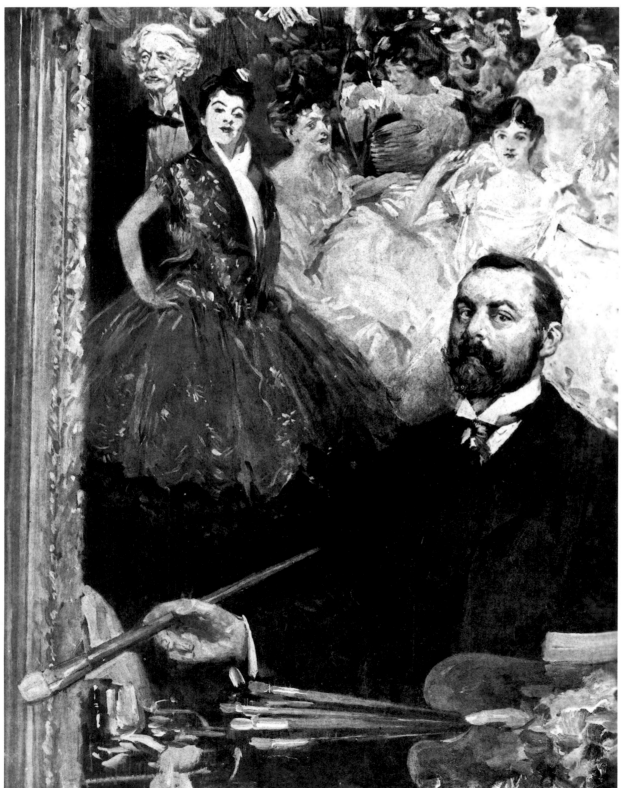

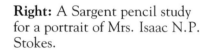

Right: A Sargent pencil study for a portrait of Mrs. Isaac N.P. Stokes.

Far right: Another pencil study by Sargent, in this case of Asher Wertheimer.

Left: A portrait (by an artist considerably less talented than his subject) of Sargent standing before some of his most famous creations.

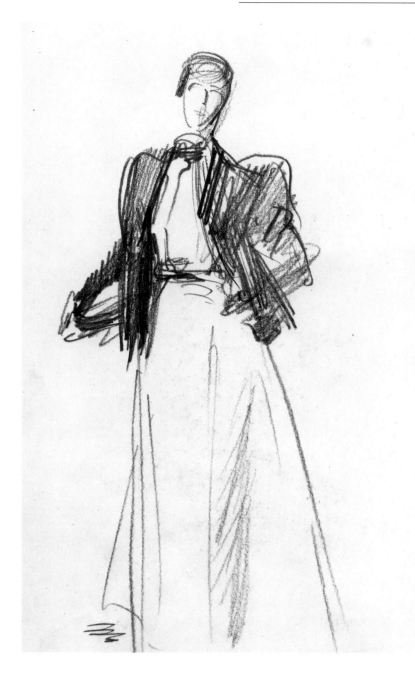

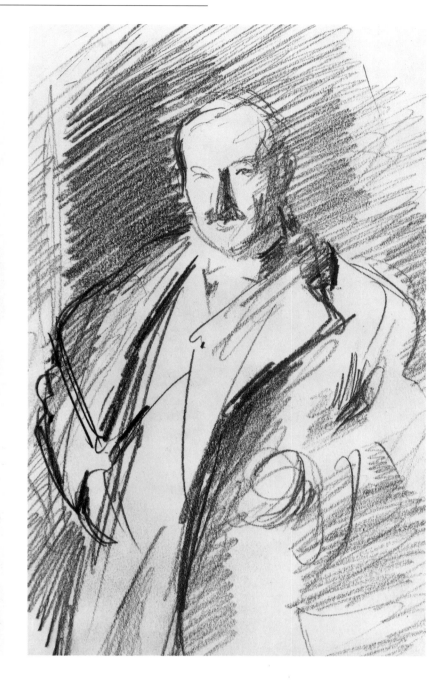

Although Sargent enjoyed teaching at the Royal Academy schools, he was occasionally dismayed to find that his pupils ignored his instructions and examples. The following passage regarding composition illustrates the excellence of his advice:

> Cultivate an ever continuous power of observation. Wherever you are, be always ready to make slight notes of postures, groups and incidents. Store up in the mind . . . a continuous stream of observations from which to make selections later. Above all things get abroad, see the sunlight and everything that is to be seen.

Sargent received praise for his portraiture of the 1890s and early 1900s from sources as revered as the London *Times* and the New York *Tribune*. Fellow artists were not always so enchanted and several of the Impressionists felt he was somewhat disloyal to their cause. Camille Pissarro commented, "As for his painting, that, of course, we can't approve of; he is not an enthusiast, but an adroit performer. . . ." This is not entirely true – Sargent was certainly in sympathy of the Impressionists. His own style – particularly in his later watercolors – reflects their influence. It seems that he adapted his talents in order to make a good living and if his portraits do not reflect the Impressionist style, it in no way diminishes their beauty or value.

A contemporary painter of the time, William Rothenstein, was a good friend of Sargent's and his portrait by Sargent done in 1897 is in the National Portrait Gallery in London. Rothenstein wrote in his *Men and Memories* of Sargent's dilemma: ". . . the disparity between his gifts and our own we were inclined to discount, by thinking we had qualities that somehow placed us among the essential artists, while he, in spite of his great gifts, remained outside the charmed circle."

Sargent was elected an associate of the National Academy of Design in New York in 1891. He had first shown work there in 1879, and during the 1890s he began to enter major competitions and shows throughout the United States. He sent nine pictures to the Columbian Exposition in Chicago in 1893 and also exhibited paintings at the Pennsylvania Academy of Fine Arts that year.

In 1890 Sargent began work on a special commission for the Boston Public Library that consisted of a series of murals for a structure designed on a grand scale. The library space measured 50,000 cubic feet and Sargent travelled to several sites in Europe, the Middle East, and northern Africa to find suitable sources of inspiration for his contributions. He visited Athens, Jerusalem, Constantinople, and Cairo in his quest and he would incorporate Egyptian gods, pagan figures, and biblical

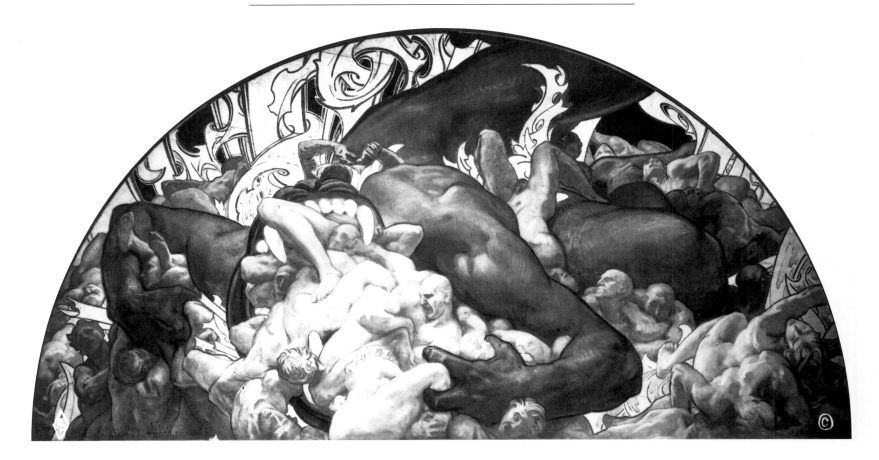

characters into his plans. These included some sculpture and bas-reliefs as well as narrative painting.

Sargent worked on the Boston Public Library decoration over a period of thirty years, having initiated his preliminary studies when he was thirty-four years old. McKim, Mead and White were the architectural firm chosen for the building. Sargent was in close contact with Charles McKim, the principal architect who oversaw the schematic development of Sargent's canvases. The artist received $15,000 for his first contract and $15,000 later for additional work.

Edwin Abbey, one of Sargent's closest friends, furnished murals for the library and Sargent also recommended Puvis de Chavannes to paint additional murals. Sargent originally focused on Spanish literature, where Abbey's interests were in the library's Shakespearean collection. After his extensive journeys, Sargent modified and added to his early ideas, influenced by the religious symbols he discovered.

Of the project, he wrote: "This Boston thing will be . . . Medieval, Spanish and religious and in my most belly-achy mood – with gold, gore and phosphorescent Hellens. What a surprise to the Community." The murals were not direct fresco painting – the canvases were applied to the walls with a white lead compound. Sargent decorated the vaulted ceiling and corridor of the special library's floor at the top of the principal staircase at the library.

He had a freedom with the murals that he did not find in portraits and preferred his library work and research to the latter. A friend, Walter Tittle, explained this in the *Illustrated London News*: "One senses it was not simply a matter of physical skills but also the ennui and pressures from patrons. The private society citizens were more likely to interfere with his work and offer critiques and suggestions." It may also have been the public recognition Sargent received for the murals.

The simplest and most memorable section of the murals is the "Frieze of the Prophets." One sees a Renaissance influence in the modelled forms of the men, whose contours recall the frescos of Giotto. These panels were painted at Edwin Abbey's studio in Gloucestershire, England (later, Sargent would lease his own studio to complete the decorations).

The remarks of one of Sargent's models for the Frieze, a young Italian named Nicola d'Inverno, were glowing: "Every hour I spent in his service will be a precious memory forever. The world calls him a great, I know him to be a good man."

A second model for the Frieze of the Prophets was poet Coventry Patmore. He was an older gentleman with a leonine head of hair, a broad forehead, beautiful eyes, and distinctive, distinguished features. The prophets Zephaniah and Obadiah on the northwest wall, Ezekiel on the north wall, Haggai on the northeast wall resemble Patmore. Hosea, Nahum, Micah, and Zachariah look like d'Inverno, and the others seem to combine features of both faces, although other models may also have been employed.

Other symbolic figures Sargent painted for the library included the Egyptian gods Osiris and Isis; the Phoenician gods Astarte, Molech, and Nut; the Pharoah and the King of Assyria. These canvases are more complex than the Frieze of the Prophets and the figures are almost obscured amid abstract detail. Their style has elements of Art Deco – a sleekness, angularity, flatness, and startling bravura. In 1901, Sargent first displayed "The Crucifix" at the Royal Academy in London before shipping the sculpture to the Boston public Library.

While he was involved with the library project, Sargent continued to send landscape paintings completed during his travels to galleries and international expositions. He won the Temple Gold Medal at the Pennsylvania Academy in 1894 and had a show of his works at Copley Hall in Boston in 1899. His travel sketches and finished oils were exhibited at the Royal Academy in London.

Sargent was offered a knighthood by the British prime minister which he declined because he did not wish to surrender his American citizenship. His reputation was established enough at this time that his work was in several public collections. He sold 83 watercolor to a museum in the United States in 1909 for £4000. In 1909 he was awarded the Order of Merit in France and the Order of Leopold in Belgium.

When World War I broke out, Sargent was in the Alps in Austria. His paintings and his companions, Adrian Stokes and his friend Colonel Armstrong, were seized and held in custody. The war was a difficult time for Sargent and he suffered deep personal losses. Both his niece, Rose-Marie, and her husband were killed in France. For most of these tumultuous years, though, Sargent was removed from the actual conflict, taking refuge in his work at the Boston Public Library and, beginning in 1916, at the Boston Museum of Fine Arts.

Classical Greek mythology was the topic Sargent decided upon for his murals at the Museum of Fine Arts. The heroic paintings of Apollo, Hercules, Minerva, and the Muses in the rotunda and on the stairway are clear and graceful images.

His sketches show the influence of Ingres whose 1914 exhibition in Paris Sargent had visited. He noted to Paul Helleu, "Ingres, Raphael and El Greco, these are now my admirations, these are what I like." In addition, Sargent mastered the special exigencies of public space. Sargent's group painting of Apollo, his followers, and the God's rearing, white chariot horses is

sculptural in its masses and boldly dramatic in its narrative. The mural of the Danaides bearing vases is exquisitely calm and elegant. These women were condemned to draw water with a sieve for eternity because they had slain their husbands. In Sargent's design they seem quiet, if not repentent about their punishment. In their forms, the viewer can also see the influence of Renaissance sculpture.

In 1917 during a visit to Florida, Sargent did several sketches of Spanish-styled mansions and native flora and fauna. In the same year he painted John D. Rockefeller's portrait. The American industrialist looks elderly, his hands are gnarled and his face is wizened yet his eyes disclose his mental acuity and he appears in full control of his empire.

By May of 1918 Sargent was back in England when the Prime Minister, Lloyd George, commissioned him to be the official British artist correspondent at the front lines. Sargent went with his friend Professor Tonks and stayed at the barracks of General Feilding near Berles au Bois, France, where he was a popular and lively dinner companion for members of the troops. Though physical circumstances were crude and uncomfortable Sargent never complained nor did he seem frightened. He set up his brushes, palette, and umbrella wherever possible.

Two of his more famous paintings of the struggle are "Gassed" and "The Generals." The first is a wonderful epic scene derived from sketches sargent collected in the field. A line of men wearing blindfolds after being gassed wander amid the bodies of other soldiers strewn on the ground writhing in pain. "The Generals" lacks this emotional content. It is a

Left top: Sargent's mural "Hell," executed for the west wall of the Boston Public Library.

Right: Part of the "Frieze of the Prophets" in the Boston Public Library. From left: Zephaniah, Joel, Obadiah and Hosea.

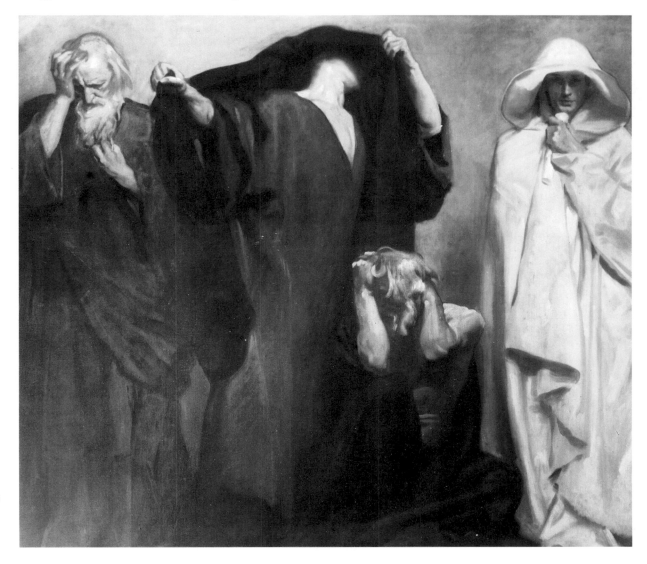

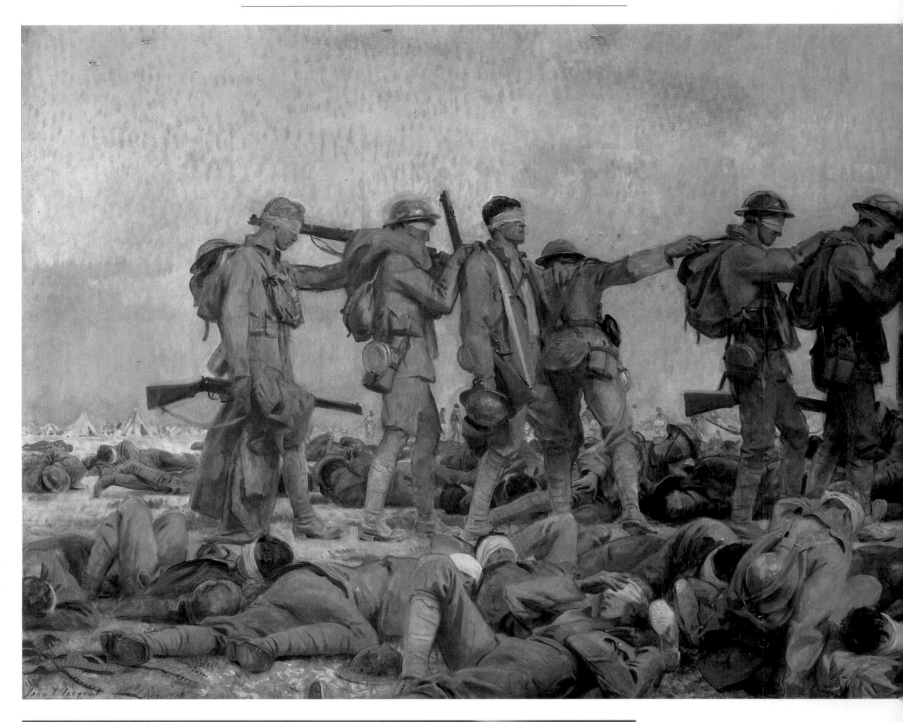

Above: Sargent's famous 1918 war painting "Gassed" hangs in the Imperial War Museum in London.

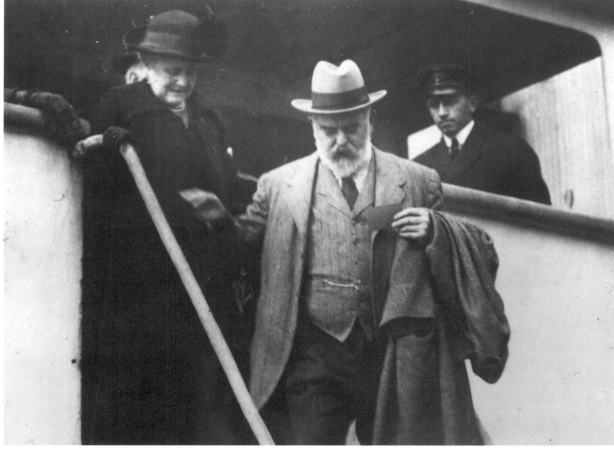

Left: Sargent at the age of 66, three years before his death, debarking from a liner in New York City.

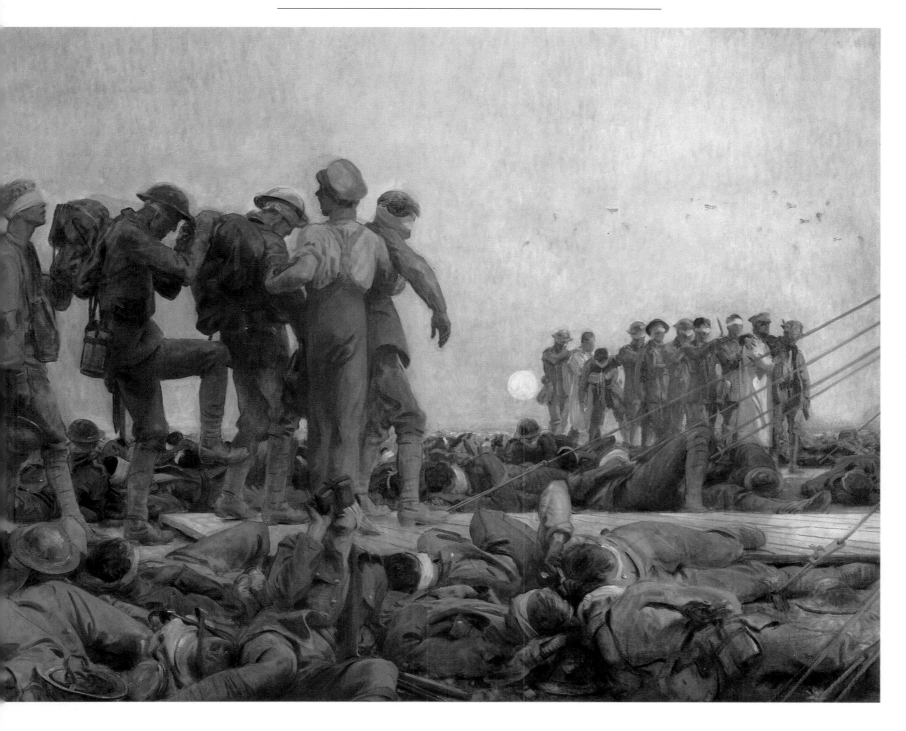

plain, horizontal array of important military figures who bear little relationship to one another. It is perfunctory and Sargent was well aware of its limitations, saying, "I am handicapped by the idea that they could never have been altogether in any particular place." Yet the painting fulfilled the requirements of his particular assignment. However, its absolute propriety and improbability lends it an amusing aspect when viewed today.

In 1922 Sargent painted two commemorative war panels for the Widener Library at Harvard University in Cambridge, Massachusetts. "The Coming of the Americans to Europe" is filled with icons of popular American culture – the eagle, the flag, and a mother and child – placed amid a phalanx of uniformed, gun-bearing soldiers. "Death and Victory" is a vivid, romantic scenario with the golden-hued, winged Nike female form of Victory being carried off by the dark, cloaked, masculine figure of Death. This painting, like several of the library canvases, echoes the Symbolist-style of the late nineteenth century that corresponded to musical effects and theatrical auras. One can imagine drum rolls and clashes of cymbals in the background.

Sargent returned to England and in July 1923 gave the address at the Royal Academy honoring the bicentenary birth of Sir Joshua Reynolds, the eighteenth-century portrait painter and first president of the Academy. Though in his late sixties, Sargent conquered his fear of speaking in public and delivered a fine lecture to an admiring audience.

He continued his vacation travels throughout the Alps and ventured to Lake O'Hara in the Canadian Rockies. Here he sketched some of his finest watercolors, sparkling with the beauty of these remote mountain climes. After his expeditions he returned to his friends and familiar surroundings in London. Here, following a farewell dinner party on the evening of April 14, 1925, with family and close associates before his departure for America, Sargent died in his sleep the next day, with a copy of Voltaire's philosophy on his bed. His intellectual powers were vital to the end.

Percy Grainger, a musician, described Sargent as "a strange mixture of a compassionate Christian and a stoical Red Indian Warrior." Yet he added, "For all these nobilities which were revealed to me in moments when I was poor and desperate enough to measure their true and rare value, I shall be unforgettably thankful as long as I have my memory."

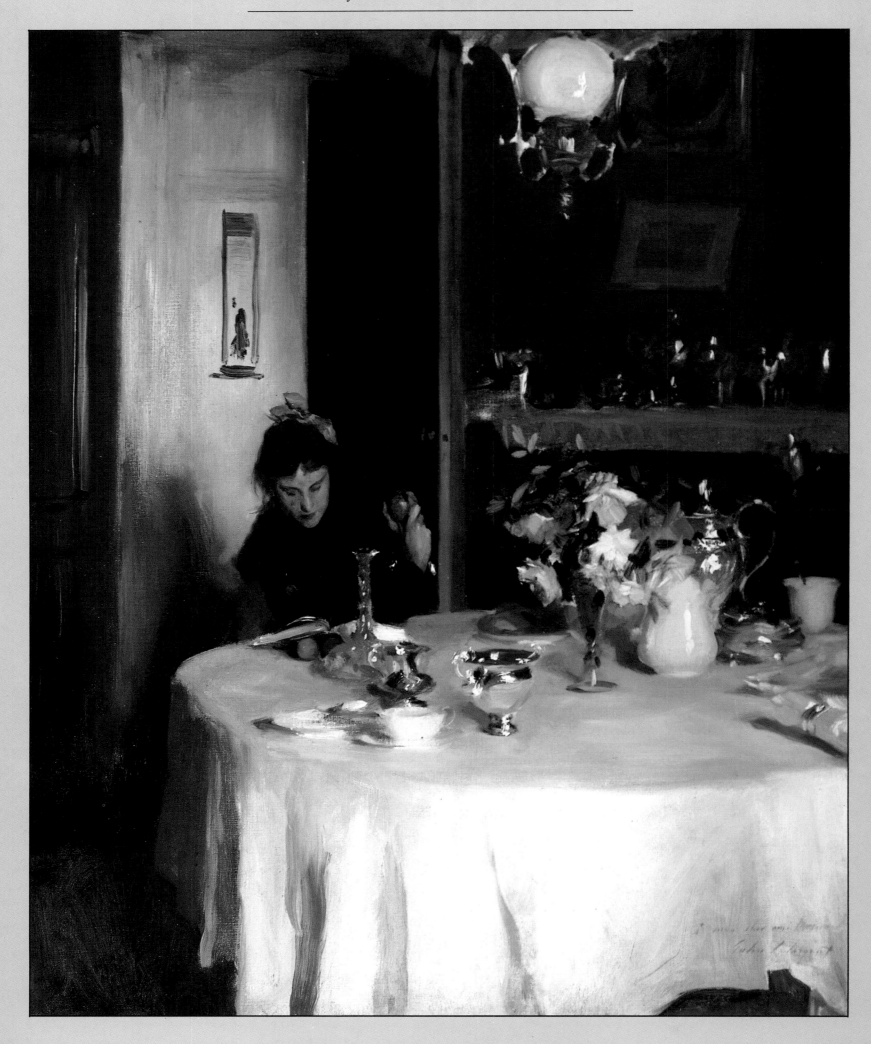

EARLY WORKS

Sargent's first oil paintings on a significant scale show the influence of his teacher, Carolus Duran, as well as a style that has an early Impressionist flavor. His 1879 portrait of Duran shows a citified dandy wearing a blouse, ruffled cuffs, and a handkerchief and carrying a brass walking stick. Duran has a full mustache in the manner of his idol, the Spanish painter Velázquez, and he has added a goatee. He looks like the social lion of mid-nineteenth century Paris so often portrayed in his own paintings.

The Sargent portraits from this period cast light upon the head, the face, and the hands of their subjects, a technique emphasized by Duran. Sargent makes brilliant use of color by simplifying the range he employs. An excellent example of this is his painting of Dr. Pozzi, dressed in a long red robe.

Symphony music was of special interest to Sargent and while in Paris he went to rehearsals at the Pas de Loup. His oil sketch of the orchestra is an active, behind the scenes perspective with a staccato technique. The style predates Raoul Dufy, though Sargent's palette is quieter and more realistic than Dufy's.

The paintings of young women from this period shows Sargent's sensitivity for the sweetness of adolescence. They also display his skill at revealing nuances of class and social bearing, though the informal sketches of peasant girls are more intriguing than the posed artifice of the society portraits. No doubt Sargent's close relationship with his sister Emily and his mother gave him a certain sympathy to paint women in the best light possible.

Sargent's paintings of the seashore at Cancale Harbor in Brittany, France, are delightful vistas of resort activities and simple pleasures found among sailboats and the fishing community. His draftsmanship is apparent in the wonderful, sleek lines of his painting "Low Tide at Cancale Harbor." Sargent's style here is similar to that of his contemporary, Degas.

The oil "Oyster Gatherers of Cancale" shows children frolicking amid the surf along the water's edge, searching for the catch of the day with baskets in hand and learning the oyster trade from the fisherwomen. The flickering light and quick brush strokes are precursors of Impressionism and remind one of Winslow Homer's paintings of Cullercoats in England from this era.

Sargent's predilection for travel can be seen in his oil sketches of Morocco and Venice. The broad, flat planes of color with which Sargent renders the stucco buildings in Morocco have an almost abstract quality that twentieth-century artists like Richard Diebenkorn would simplify several degrees further.

The paintings of Venice have an air of mystery — street corners and interiors where the light is dim and the characters wear cloaks and dark clothing. Suggestion of form takes precedence over fixed detail, and the figures' vertical shapes echo the tall, narrow buildings surrounding them. Black and white are the predominant hues whose contrast is used to dramatic and subtle effect.

Sargent's travels to Spain in 1879 and 1880 gave him a feeling for the vibrant, volatile nature of Spanish dancing and a love of Spanish music. He combined the essence of both of these in his masterpiece, "El Jaleo" of 1882. Gypsy dancers, guitar players, castanets, ruffled skirts, and the excitement of an evening in a Spanish cabaret are featured here. The passion and brio of a nationality come forth in this painting.

Left:
The Breakfast Table
1884, oil on canvas, 21¾×18¼ in.
Bequest of Grenville L. Winthrop,
Courtesy of Fogg Art Museum, Harvard University, Cambridge, MA
(1943.150)

Overleaf:
The Oyster Gatherers of Cancale
1877, oil on canvas, 16¼×23¾ in.
Gift of Mary Appleton,
© *Museum of Fine Arts, Boston, MA*
(35.708)

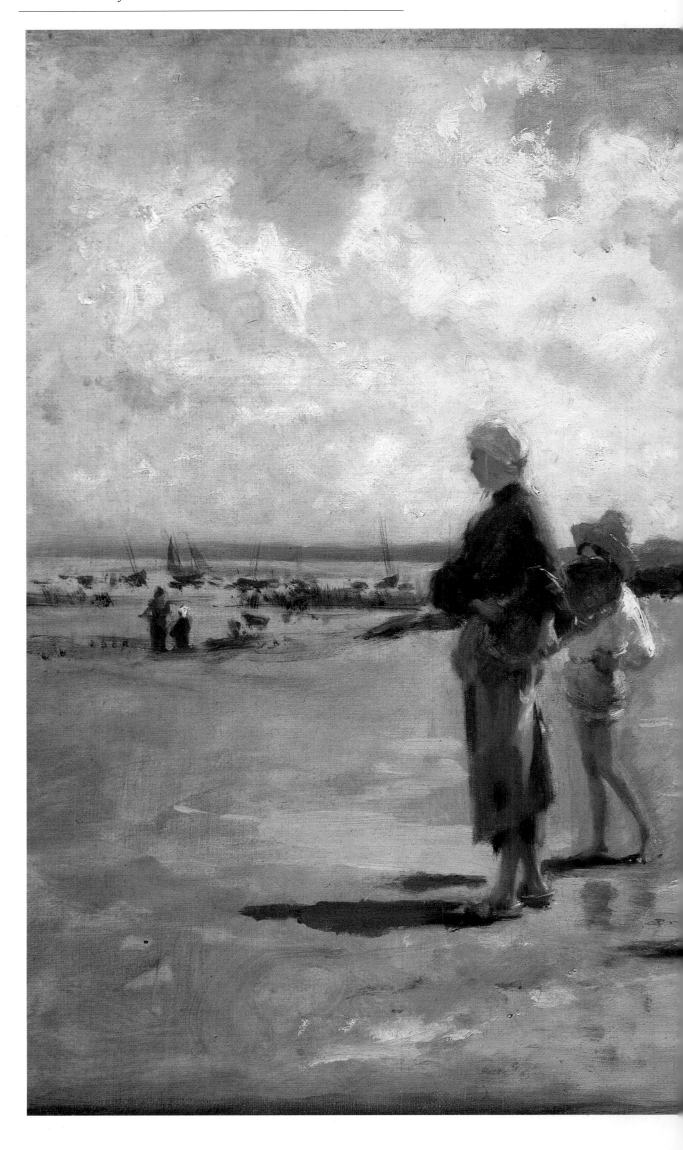

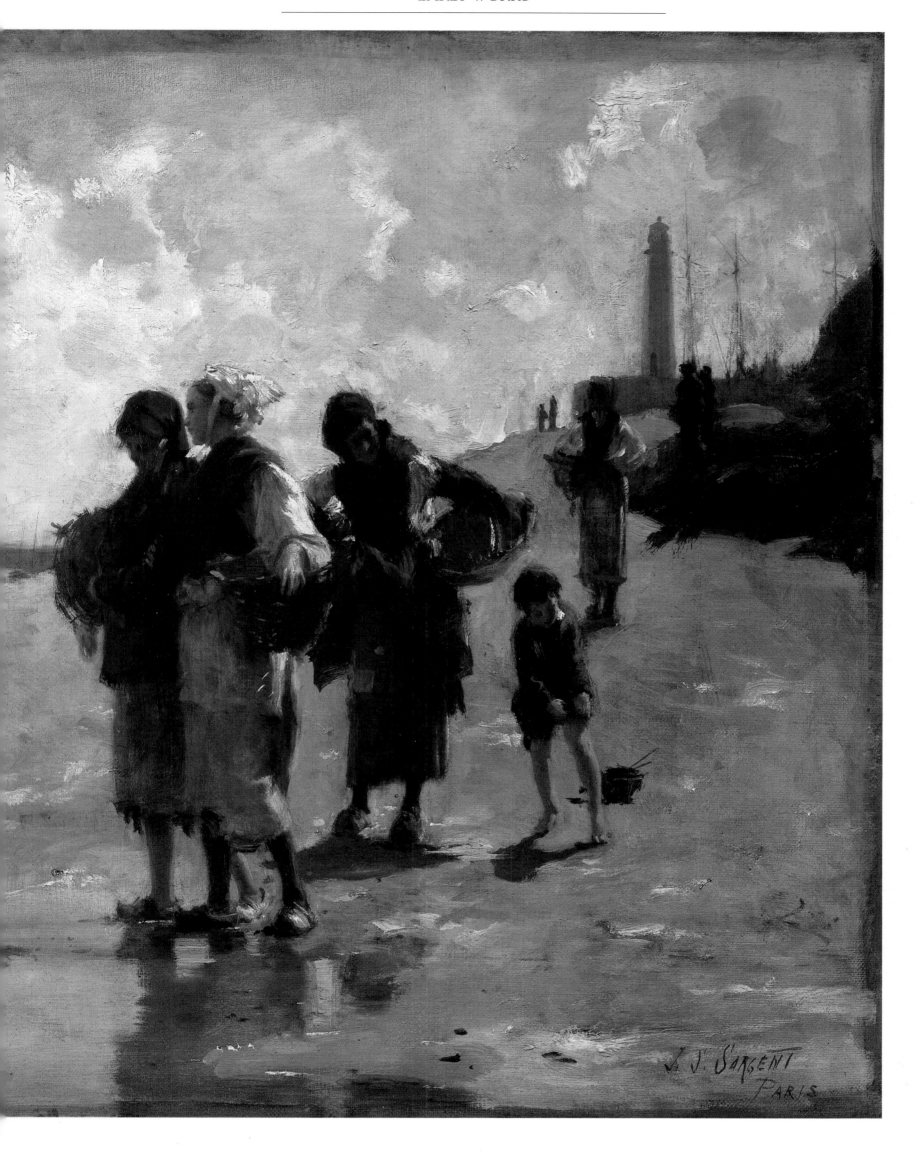

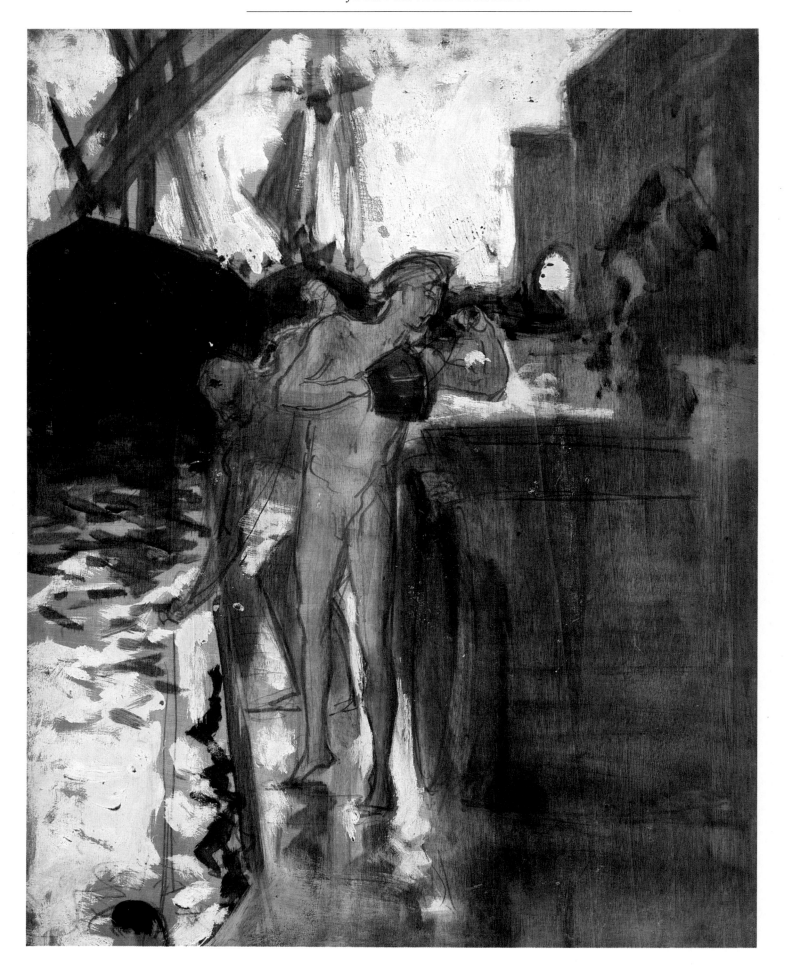

Two Nude Bathers Standing on a Wharf
1880, oil on wood, 13¾×10½ in.
Gift of Mrs. Francis Ormond,
The Metropolitan Museum of Art, New York, NY
(50.130.10)

Right:
Rehearsal of the Pasdeloup Orchestra at the Cirque d'Hiver
1876, oil on canvas, 21¾×13¼ in.
Charles Henry Hayden Fund,
The Museum of Fine Arts, Boston, MA
(22.598)

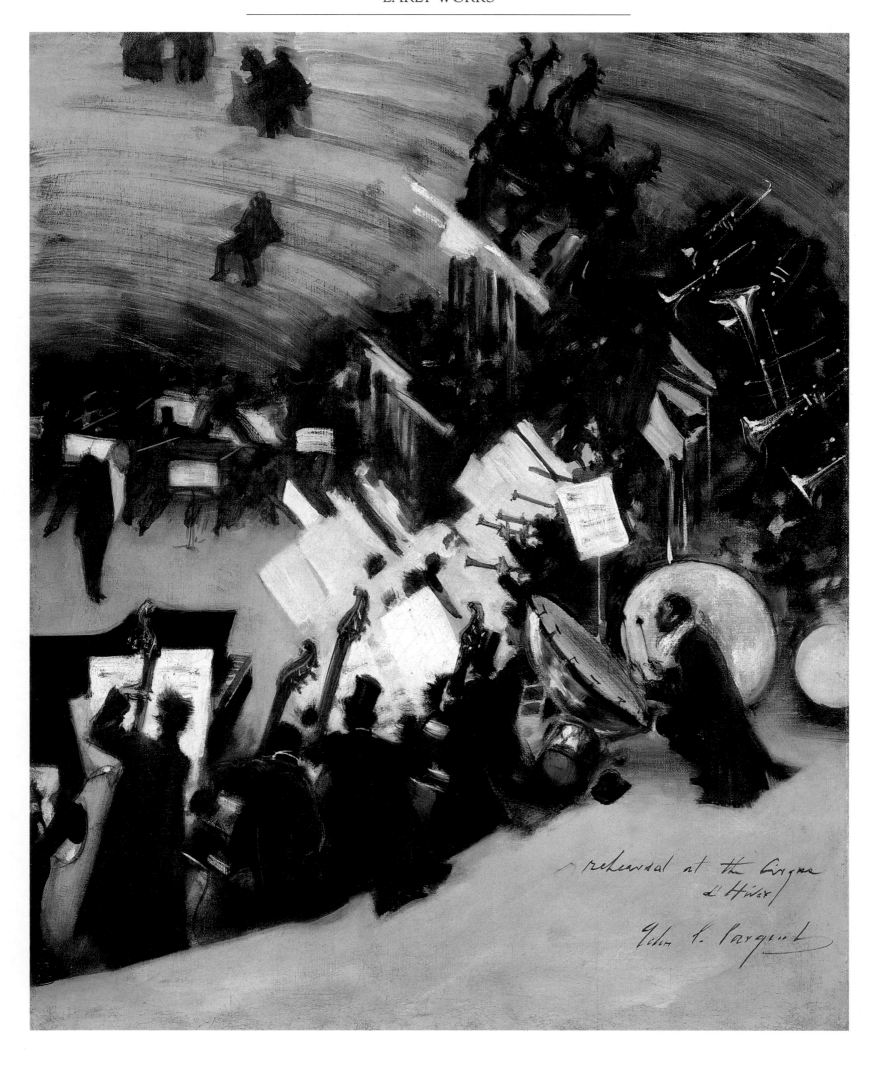

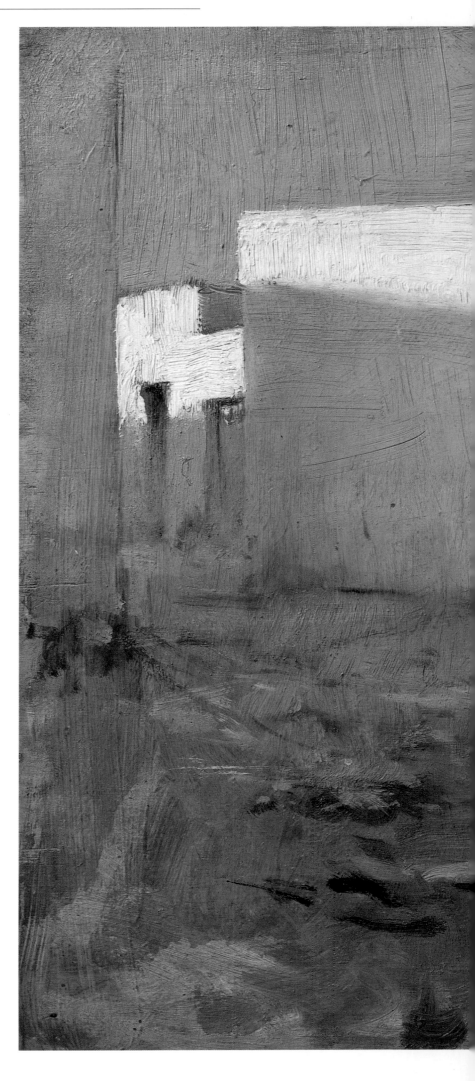

Moorish Buildings in Sunlight
1879-80?, oil on wood, 10¼×13⅞ in.
Gift of Mrs. Francis Ormond, 1950,
The Metropolitan Museum of Art, New York, NY
(50.130.9)

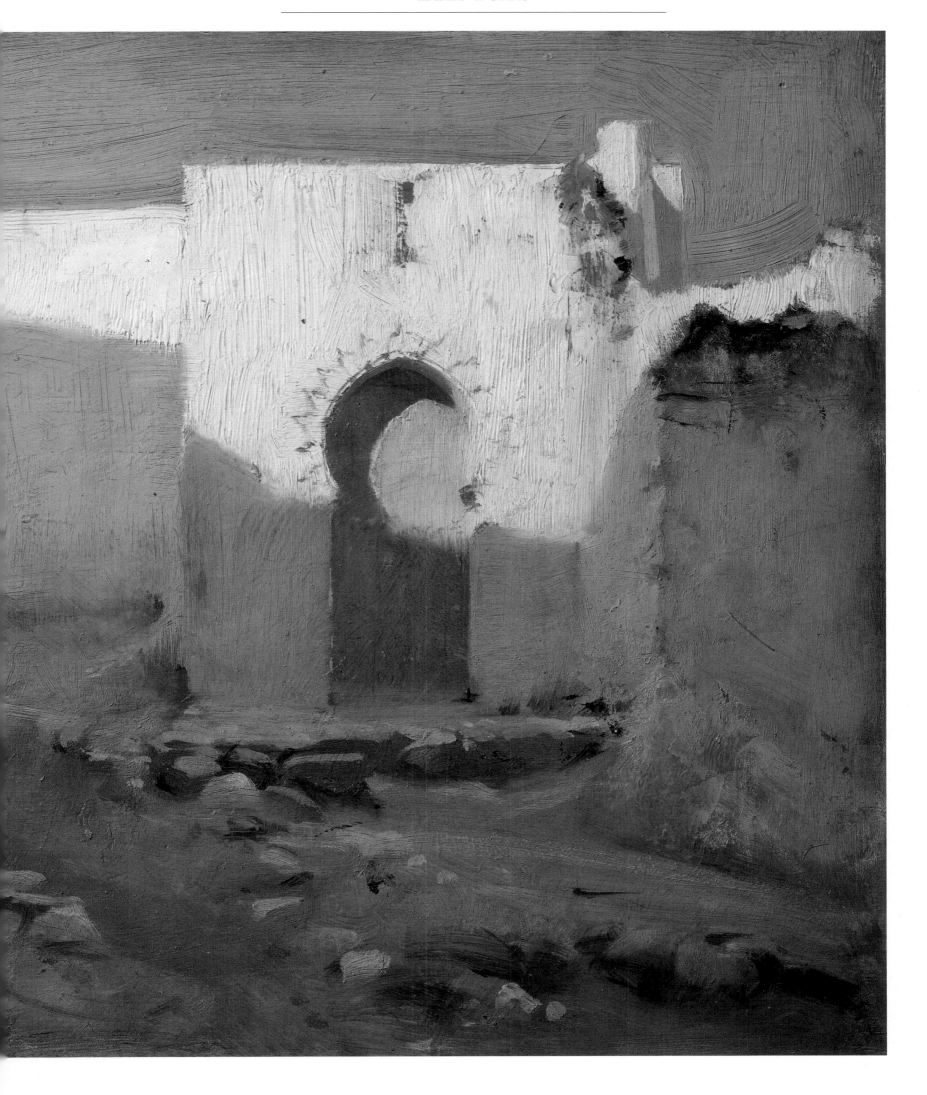

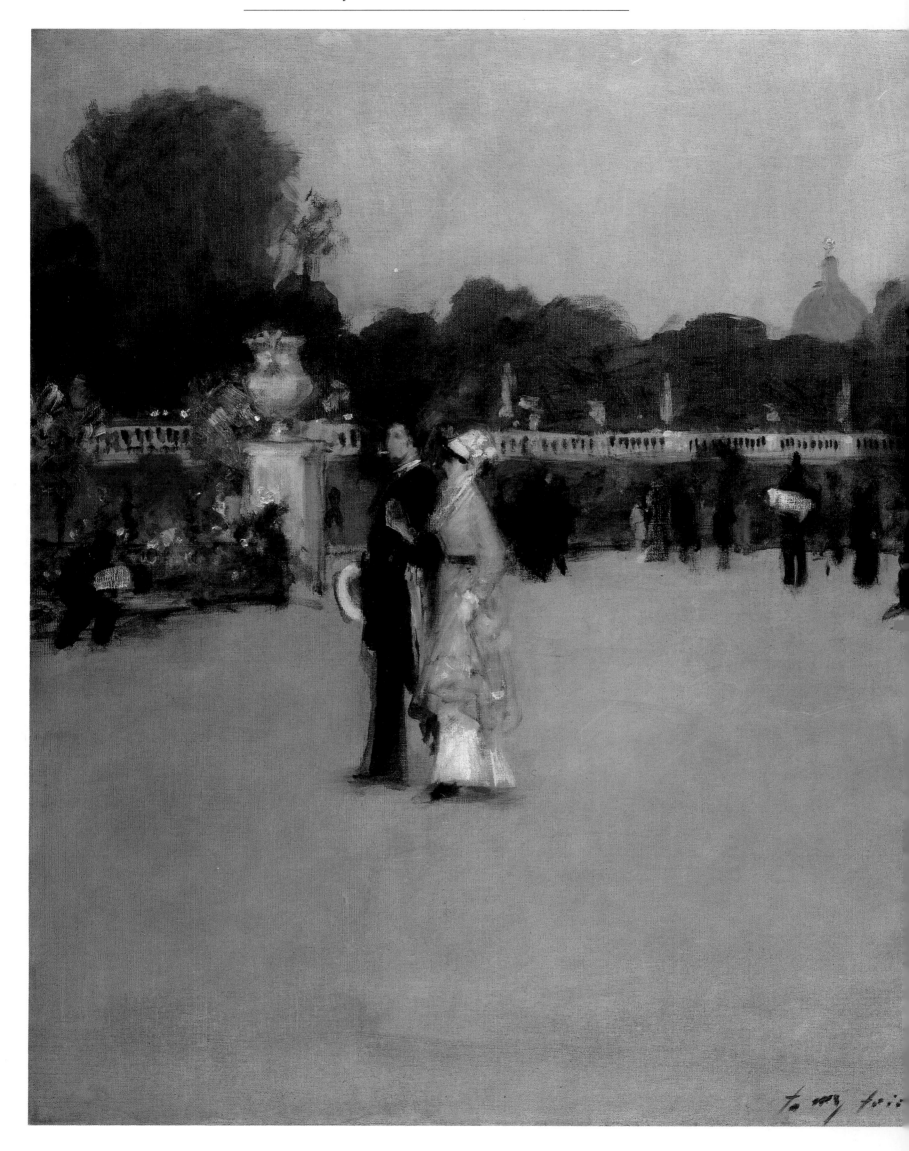

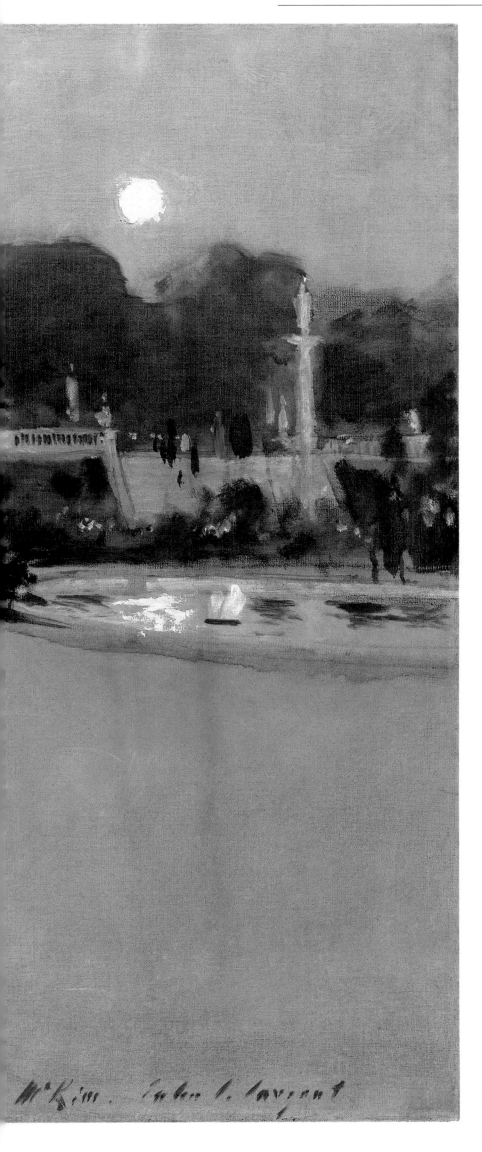

The Luxembourg Gardens at Twilight
1879, oil on canvas, 29×36½ in.
Gift of the Martin B. Koon Memorial Collection,
The Minneapolis Institute of Arts, MN
(16.20)

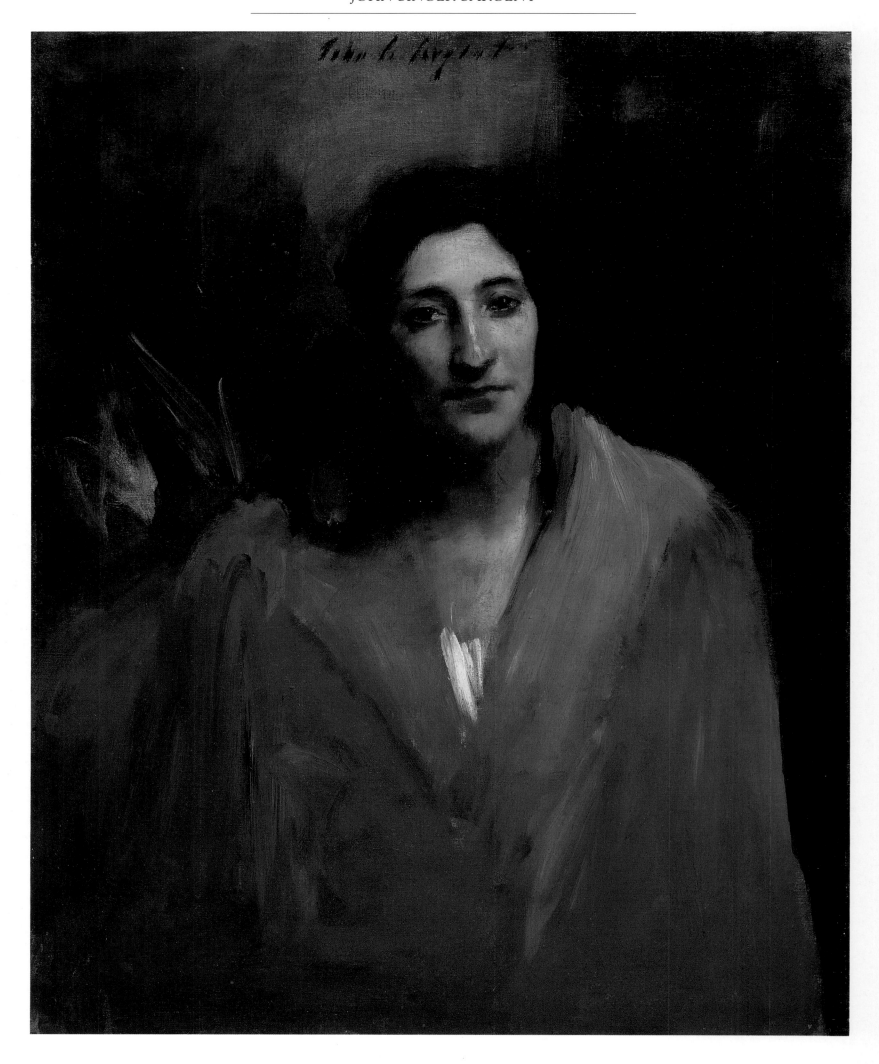

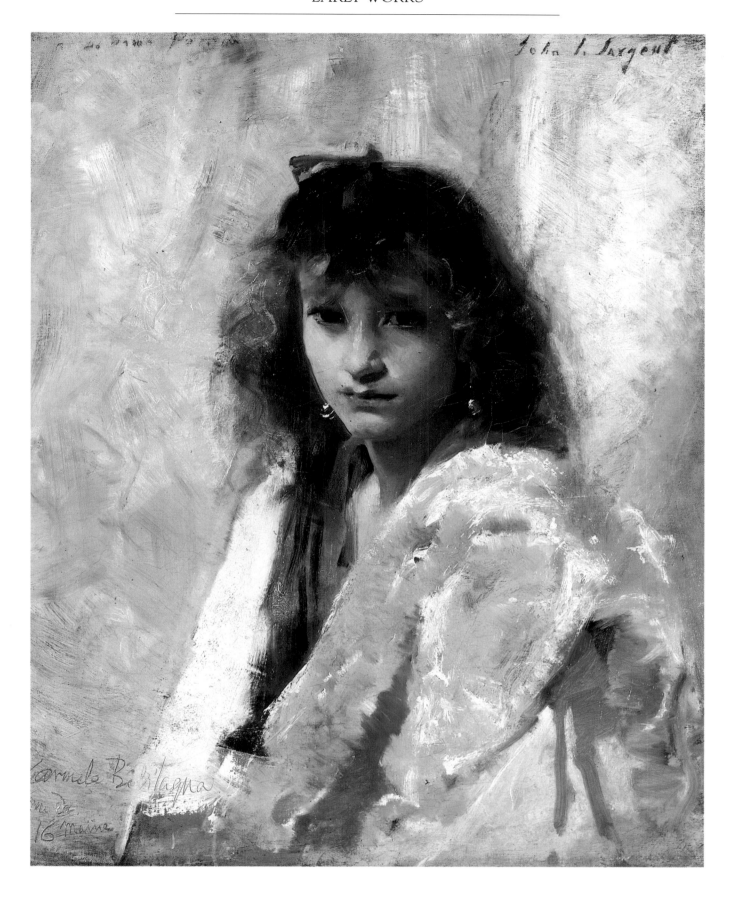

Left:
Gitana
1876, oil on canvas, 29×23⅝ in.
Gift of George A. Hearn, 1910,
The Metropolitan Museum of Art, New York, NY
(10.64.10)

Carmela Bertagna
ca. 1880, oil on canvas, 23½×19½ in.
Bequest of Frederick W. Schumacher,
Columbus Museum of Art, OH
([57] 43.11)

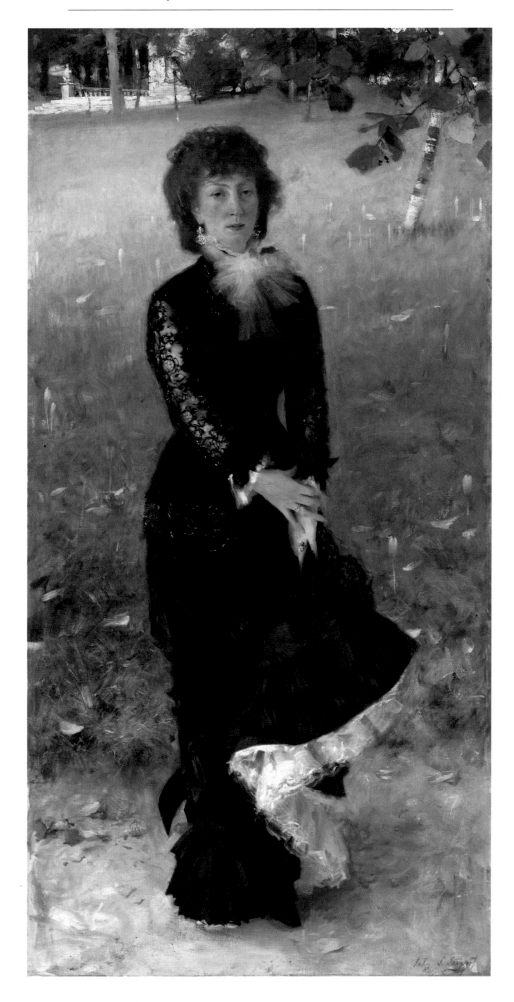

Madame Edouard Pailleron
1879, oil on canvas, 82×39½ in.
Gift of Katharine McCook Knox, John A. Nevius,
Mr. and Mrs. Lansdell K. Christie,
The Corcoran Gallery of Art, Washington, DC

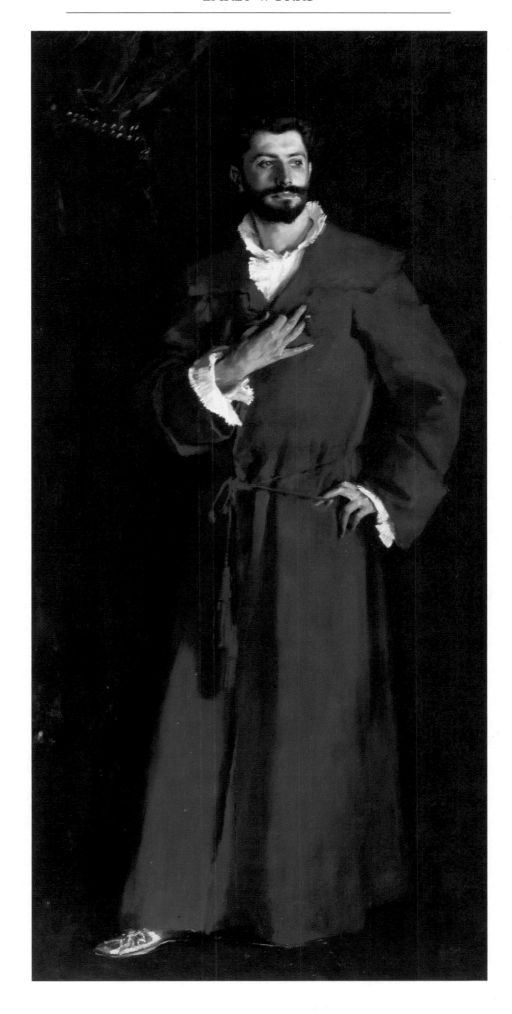

Doctor Pozzi at Home
1881, oil on canvas, 80½×43⅞ in.
The Armand Hammer Foundation, Los Angeles, CA

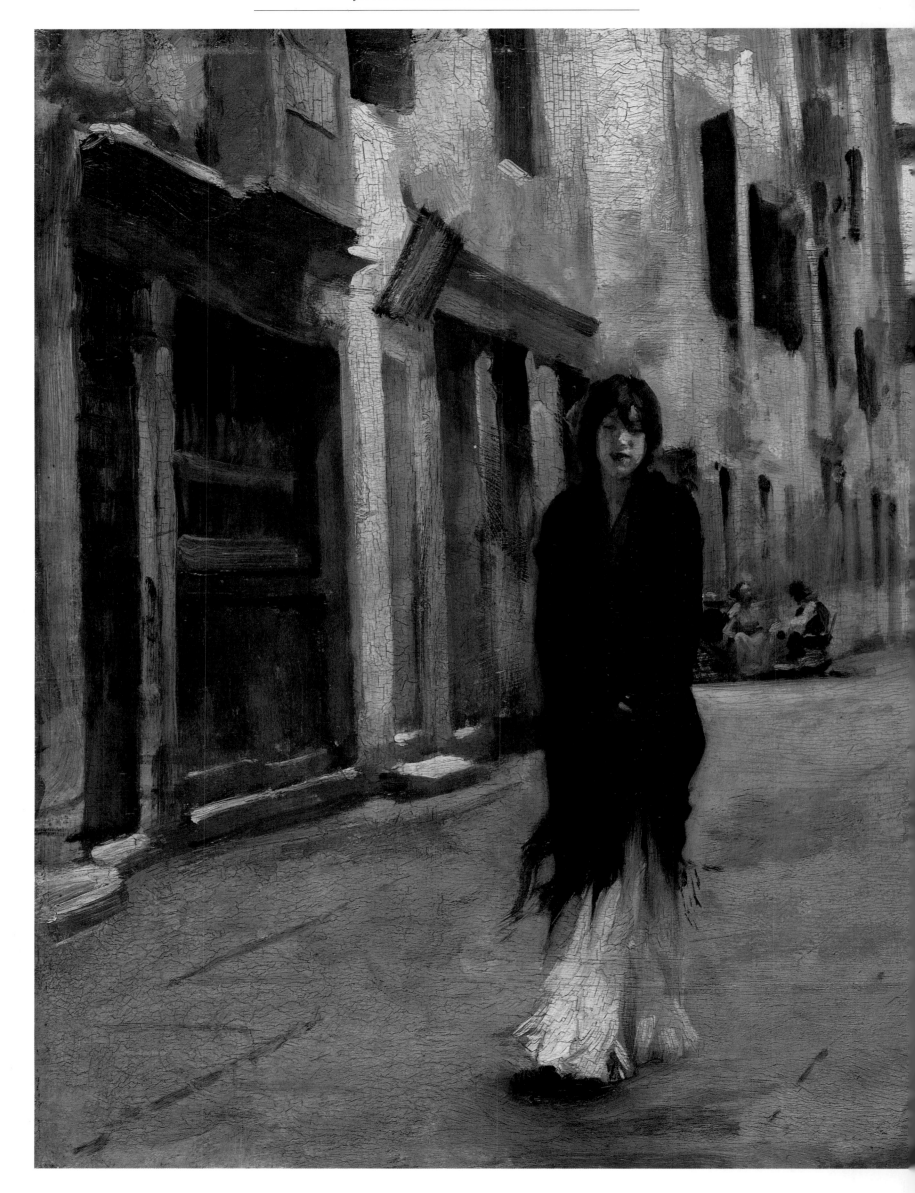

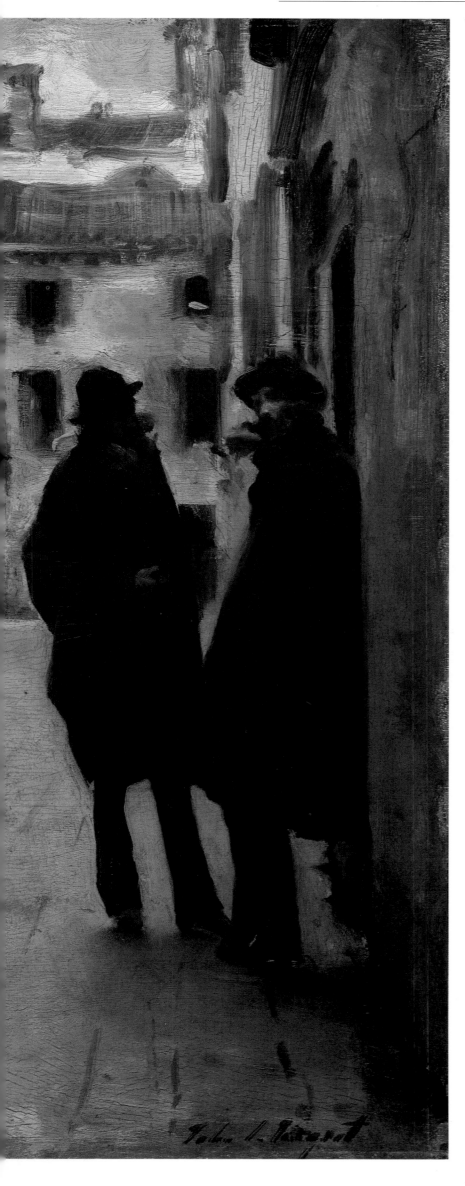

Street in Venice
1882, oil on wood, 17¾×21¼ in.
Gift of the Avalon Foundation,
National Gallery of Art, Washington, DC
(1962.4.1)

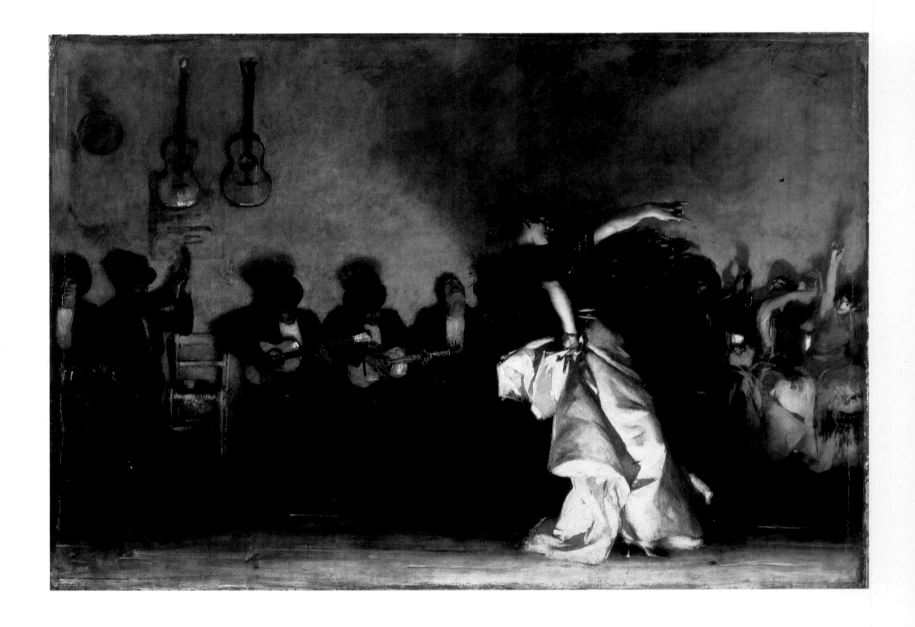

El Jaleo
1882, oil on canvas, 94½×137 in.
Isabella Stewart Gardner Museum/Art Resource, New York, NY
(256G)

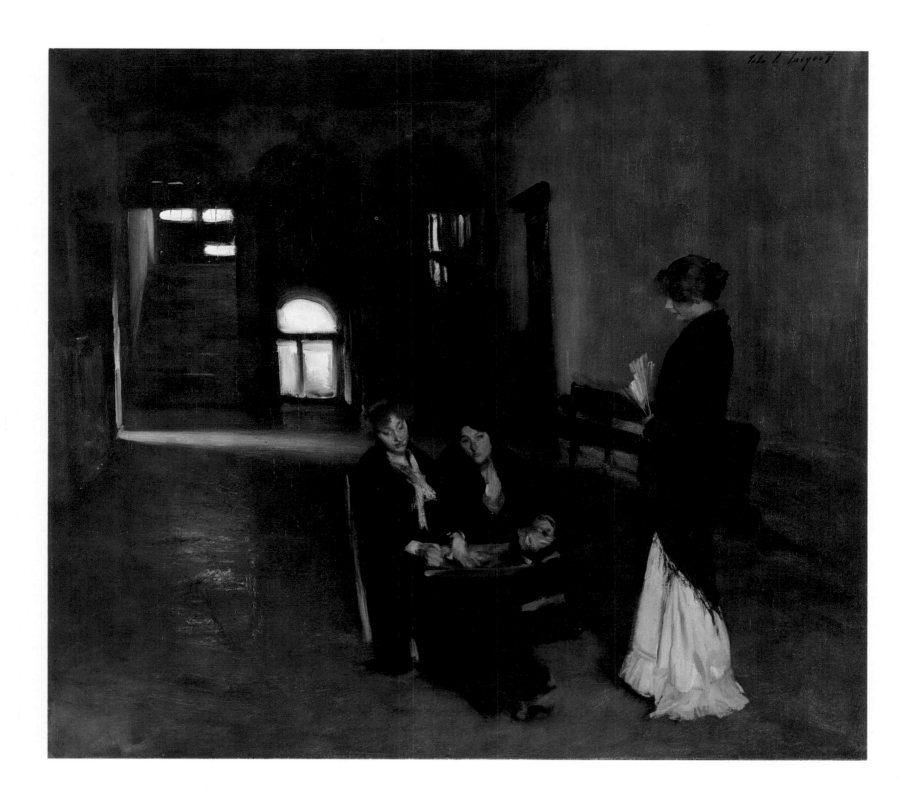

Venetian Bead Stringers
c. 1880-82, oil on canvas, 26⅜×30¾ in.
Friends of the Albright Art Gallery Fund, 1916,
Albright-Knox Art Gallery, Buffalo, NY

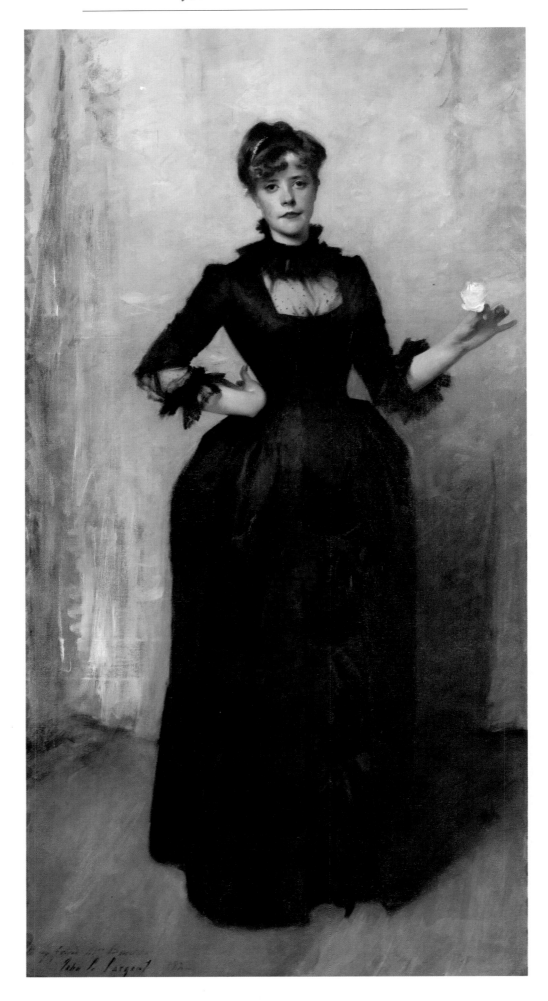

Lady With the Rose (Charlotte Louise Burckhardt, 1862-1892)
1882, oil on canvas, 84×44¾ in.
Bequest of Mrs. Valerie B. Hadden, 1932,
The Metropolitan Museum of Art, New York, NY
(32.154)

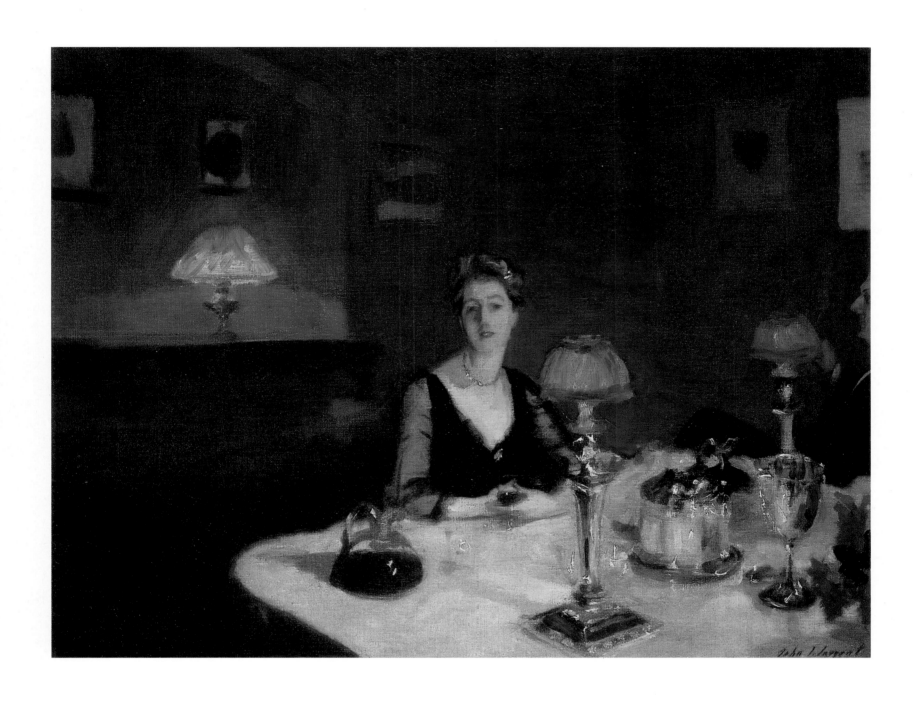

A Dinner Table at Night (The Glass of Claret)
1884, oil on canvas, 20¼×26¼ in.
Gift of the Atholl McBean Foundation,
The Fine Arts Museums of San Francisco, CA
(73.12)

Overleaf:
Reapers Resting in a Wheatfield
1885, oil on canvas, 28×36 in.
Gift of Mrs. Francis Ormond,
The Metropolitan Museum of Art, New York, NY
(50.130.14)

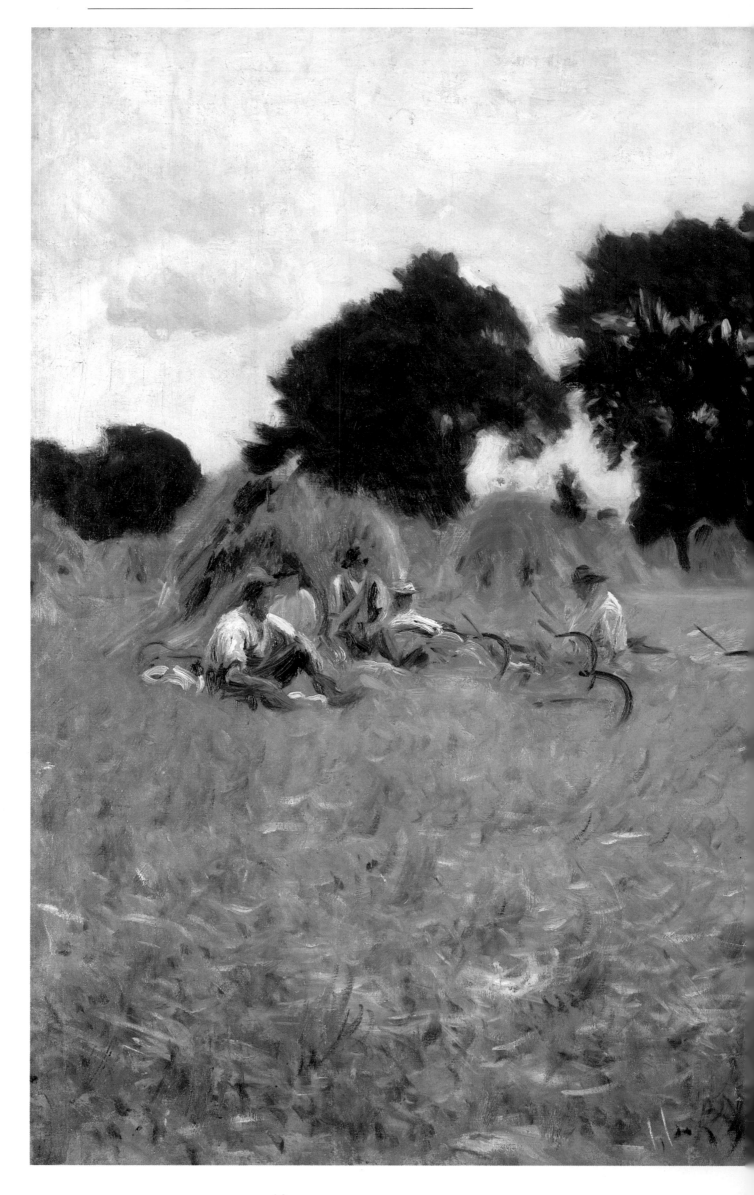

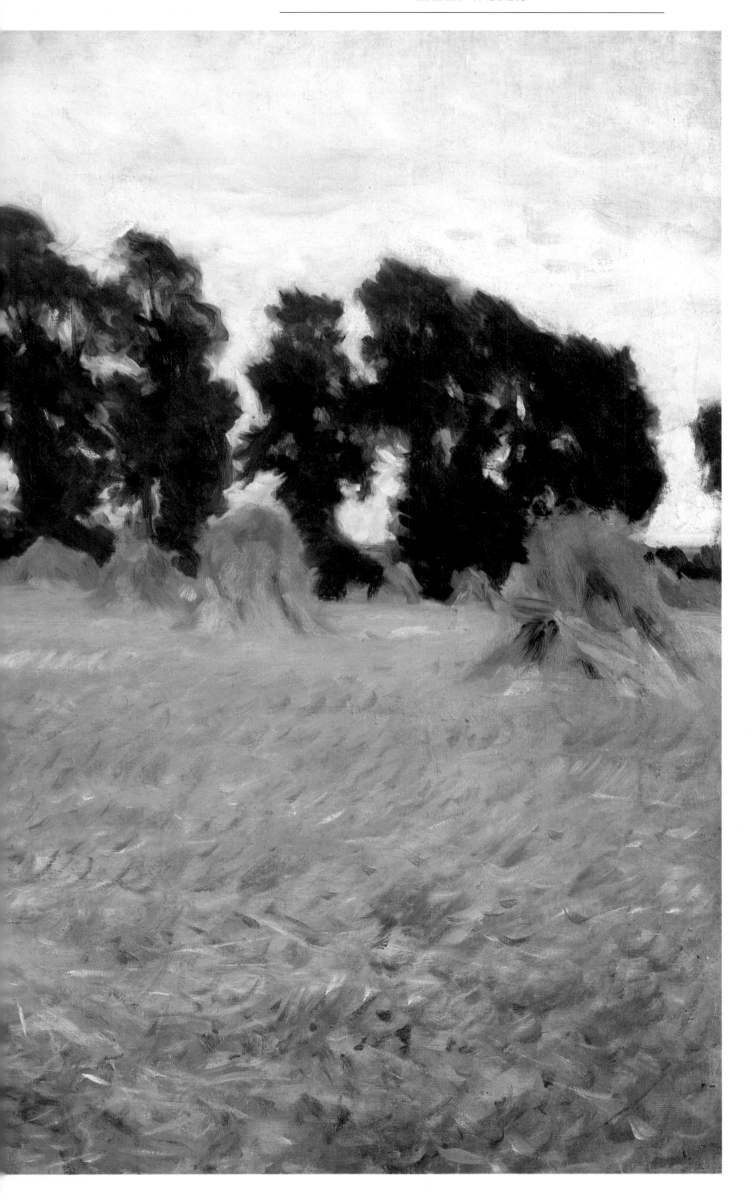

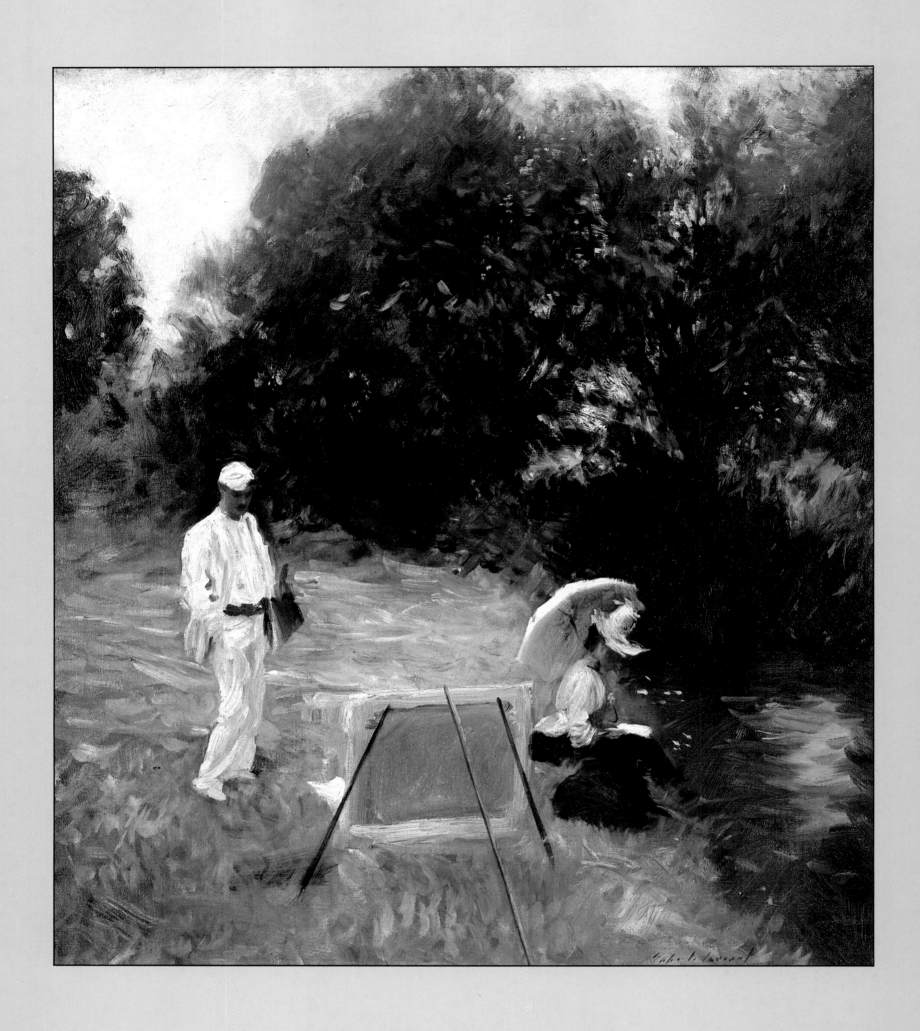

Dennis Miller Bunker Painting at Calcot
c. 1888, oil on canvas, 26¾×25 in.
© *Daniel J. Terra Collection,*
Terra Museum of American Art, Chicago, IL
(36.1980)

Friends and
Fellow Artists

The varied sketches and portraits Sargent painted of his colleagues, relatives, and acquaintances during the 1880s and 1890s express a freedom and show a lively brush-stroke style different from the finished, polished effect required by his society patrons. They are more impressionistic, perhaps because of his close association with Claude Monet at this time.

Sargent's friends were writers and artists, many of them Americans abroad. He numbered among his associates Robert Louis Stevenson, Henry James, William Merritt Chase, Oscar Wilde, and several other people less well-known today, including Ralph Curtis, Paul Helleu, and Dennis Miller Bunker.

There are several paintings of excursions along the Avon and the Thames in England, boating parties, and moments of reverie by the riverbanks near Broadway where Sargent resided during the summer months.

Sargent painted his friends at work with brushes and palettes in hand, often accompanied by their wives. These suggest leisure as well, with a canoe or fishing rod strategically placed to set up horizontal and vertical planes on a particular canvas. Sargent balanced the different masses in his paintings in this way. Thus a portrait of his sister in a long, white dress would create a strong vertical focus – the horizontal thrust would be indicated by the slim, dark fishing rod she held.

Color was another element Sargent used to highlight his subject. A painting of his friend, Paul Helleu, sketching, is set in a field of maize, pale green, and ecru brush strokes. A scarlet red canoe traversing the diagonal livens the entire work and draws attention to Helleu's wife's bright lips and the touches of carmine in the palette.

The alert expression in the eyes of Robert Louis Stevenson in Sargent's portrait reveals the keen intelligence of the writer. He is presented in a casual pose sitting in a wicker chair and smoking a cigarette. Every gesture is lean and long-limbed. The lightest, brightest, and most clearly focused portions of the canvas are Stevenson's face and hands. Though the rest of the painting is impressionistic, here Sargent capitalizes on his classical training.

A quick, small oil sketch of Ralph Curtis, Sargent's friend and fellow American artist, was painted while the two were on vacation in the Netherlands. It is a wonderful, fresh rendering. Only Curtis's bowler hat, silver-tipped walking stick and the spats on his feet give away the era of the painting. Curtis appears dapper in spirit and almost elfin as he is tucked beside the sand dunes. His soft, green suit is like camouflage against the seagrass.

Sargent was a great admirer of Claude Monet and worked side by side with the French painter at Giverny in the late 1880s. In 1887 he bought one of Monet's paintings and wrote to him the following paean: 'I. . . I rest before it for entire hours in a state of rapturous delight . . . or enchantment if you prefer. I am thrilled to have at my home a true source of pleasure."

Photographs, sketches, and caricatures of Sargent by his friends during the London years are witty testimony to his physical demeanor and are affectionate portraits of the artist. When he went out in the fields in the Cotswolds countryside near Broadway to paint, he wore a straw boater, checkered vest, tie, and casual white slacks. He carried a basket along to hold his brushes, palette, and paints. In profile he looks remarkably similar to his oil painting of Claude Monet of 1887. Both men had full dark beards and mustaches, short-cropped hair, and intent gazes.

Max Beerbohm's caricature of the artist at his 31 Tite Street residence in London shows the citified aspect of Sargent's personality. Sargent is dressed in a dark suit, looks prosperously portly and tosses his head back, casually smoking. He might be enjoying repartee at a cocktail party. In fact, Sargent was quite uncomfortable at social gatherings and disliked speaking in public. When asked to deliver a speech at Harvard University, he declined, remarking in his letter to the university, "The miracle of overcoming something like panic when asked to speak has never happened to me yet . . . ."

Sargent was a loyal and devoted friend and though he spoke haltingly, he wrote beautifully and with conviction about young artists he supported. When his friend, Robert Brough, was critically injured he rushed to his side to visit him. Brough died soon after and Sargent wrote this introduction to a catalogue of Brough's paintings on display: "The developing of this natural gift into a perfectly supple and practised medium seems to be the direction in which his progress can best be traced when one follows it through the interesting series of portraits that are now gathered together in tribute to his memory."

Sargent's portrait of Henry James of 1913 shows the writer's critical expression, his ample proportions and his adopted stuffy British upper-class mannerisms. It also gives one a sense of James's articulate intelligence. James's analysis of Sargent's paintings discloses the slightly dissatisfied nature of the novelist: "His talent is brilliant but there is a certain incompleteness in it, in his extremely attaching nature, a certain want of seriousness." Despite James's misgivings, Sargent was a great success in London and would soon attain more prestige, and attendant demands for portraits, than any other artist living there at the time.

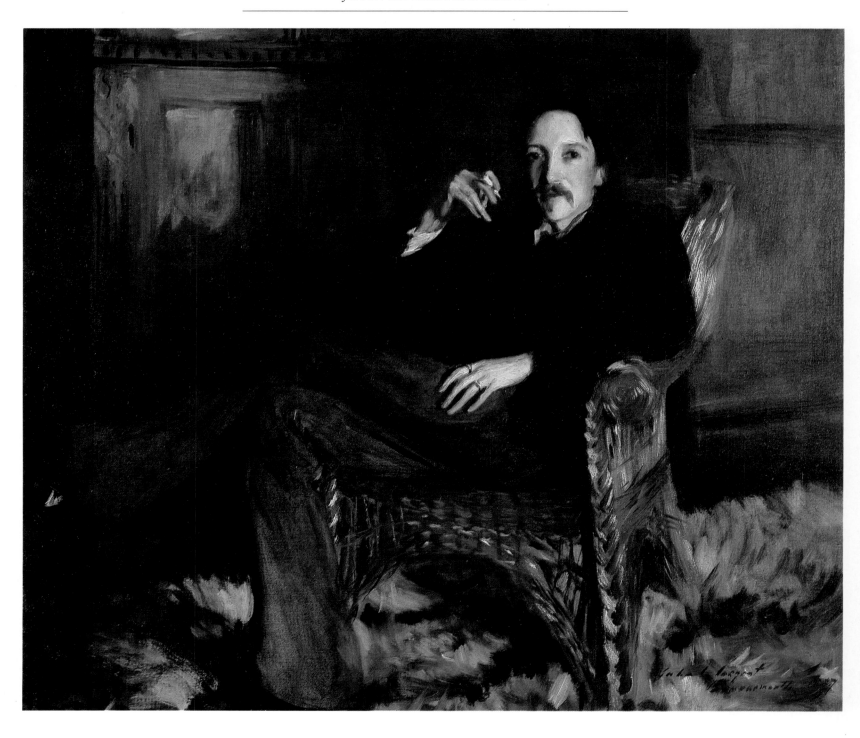

Robert Louis Stevenson
1887, oil on canvas, 20 1/16 × 24 5/16 in.
Bequest of Mr. and Mrs. Charles Phelps Taft,
The Taft Museum, Cincinnati, OH
(1931.472)

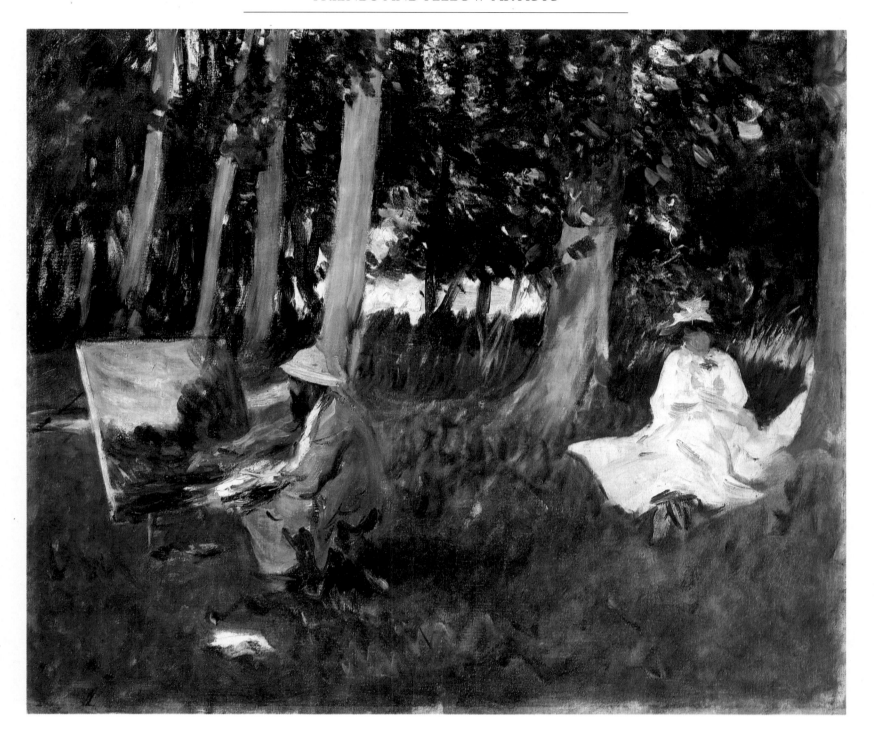

Claude Monet Painting at the Edge of a Wood
1887-89, oil on canvas, 21¼×25½ in.
The Tate Gallery, London/Art Resource, New York, NY
(N4103)

Portrait of Ralph Curtis on the Beach at Scheveningen
1880, oil on board, 17⅝×20⅞ in.
Gift of the Walter Clay Hill and Family Foundation,
Collection: High Museum of Art, Atlanta, GA
(73.3)

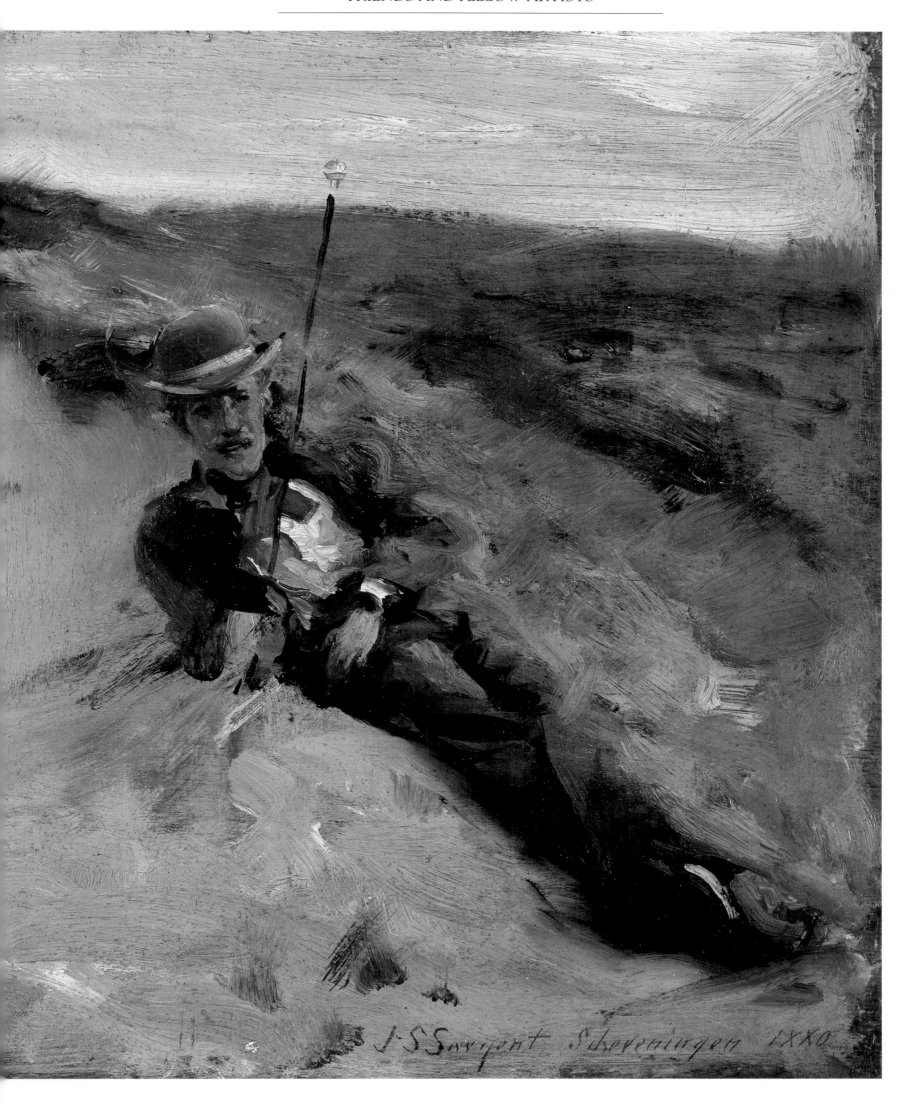

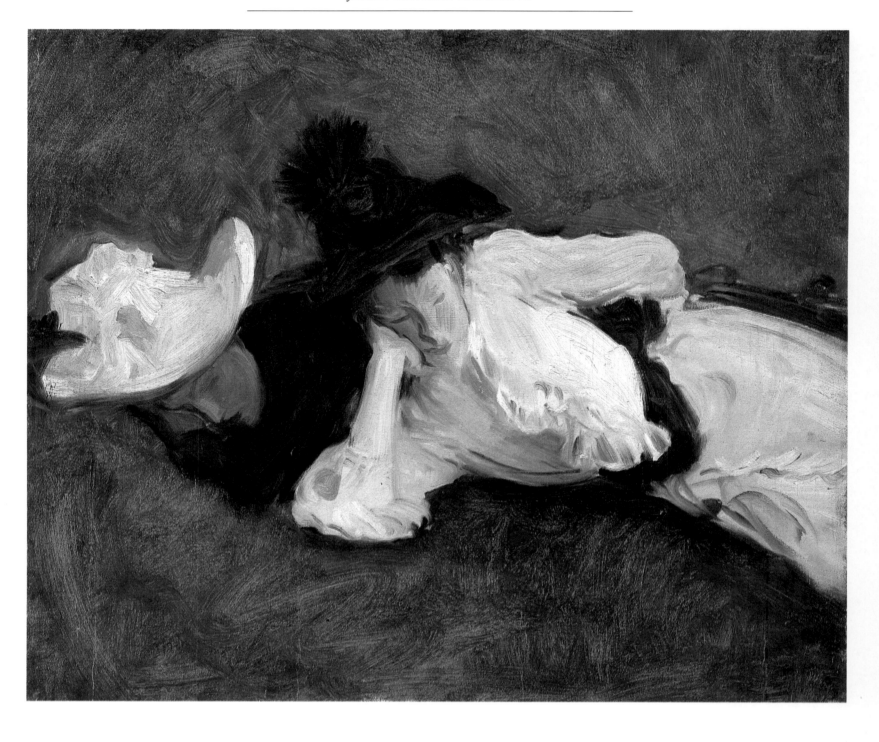

Two Girls on a Lawn
c. 1889, oil on canvas, 21⅛×25¼ in.
Gift of Mrs. Francis Ormond, 1950,
The Metropolitan Museum of Art, New York, NY
(50.130.20)

Right:
Two Girls With Parasols at Fladbury
1889, oil on canvas, 29½×25 in.
Gift of Mrs. Francis Ormond, 1950,
The Metropolitan Museum of Art, New York, NY
(50.130.13)

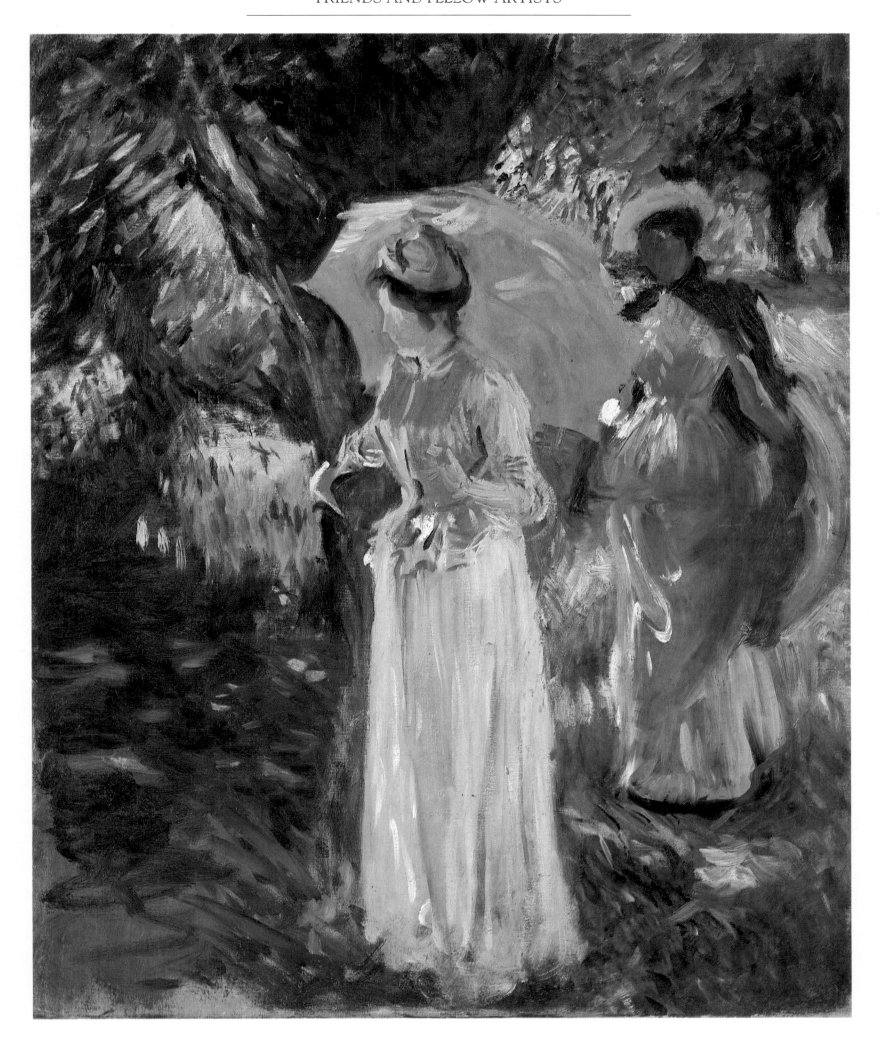

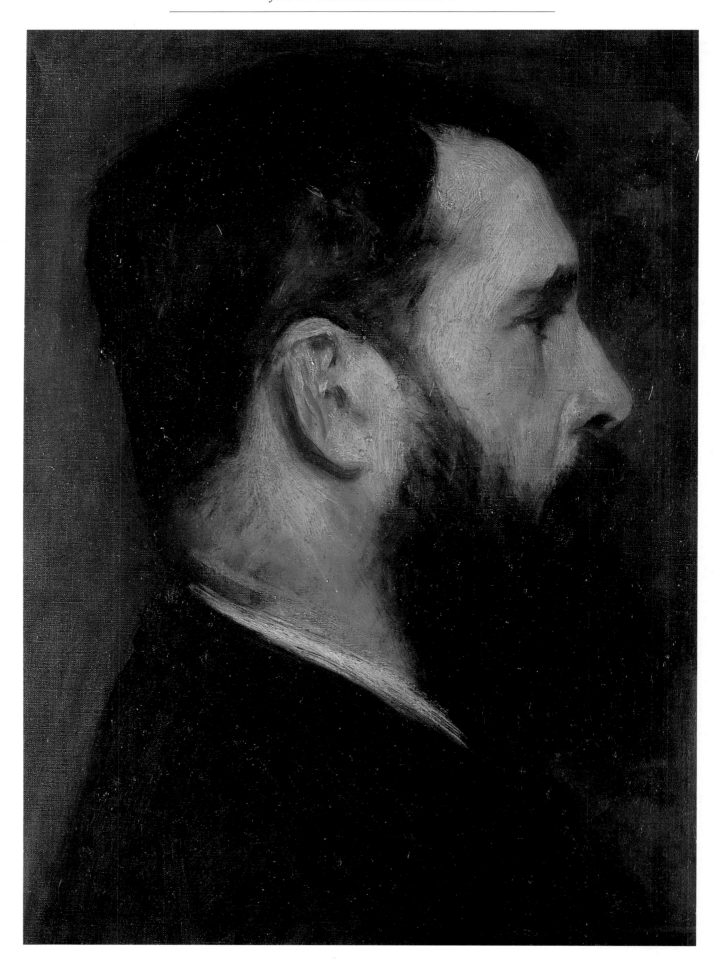

Portrait of Claude Monet
1889, oil on canvas, 16×13 in.
Collection: National Academy of Design, New York, NY
(1123)

Right:
Madame Paul Poirson
1885, oil on canvas, 59×33½ in.
Mr. and Mrs. Richard A. Manoogian, Beatrice Rogers,
Gibbs-Williams, and Ralph H. Booth Funds,
Founders Society, Detroit Institute of Arts, MI

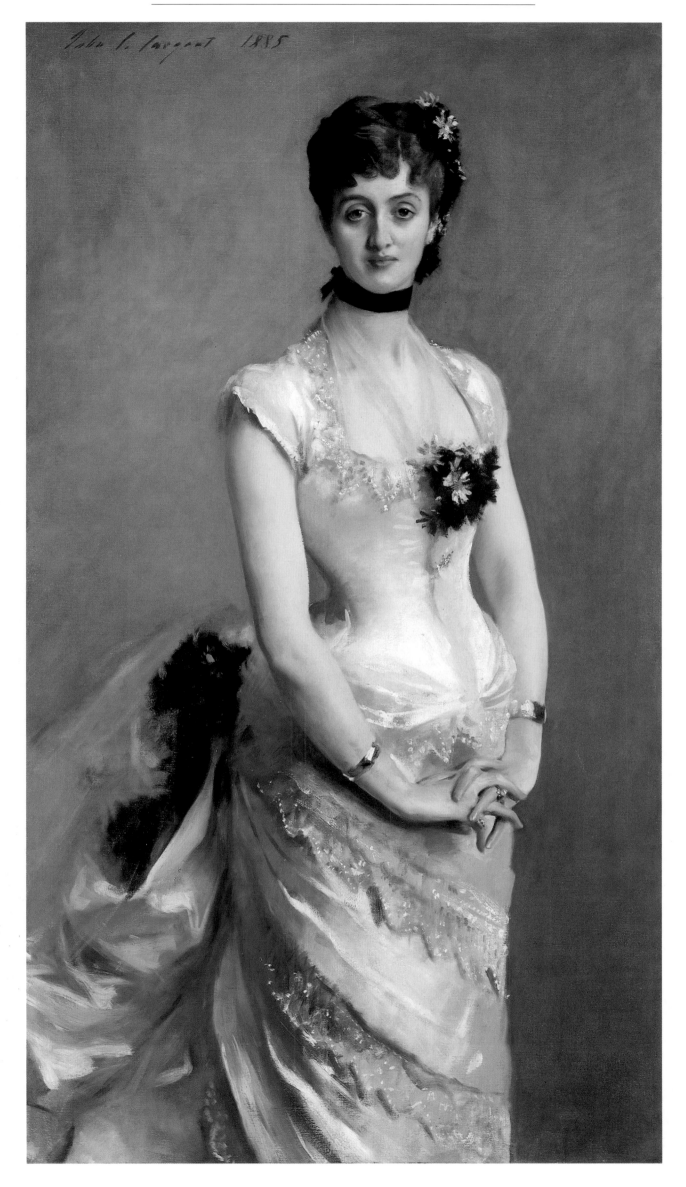

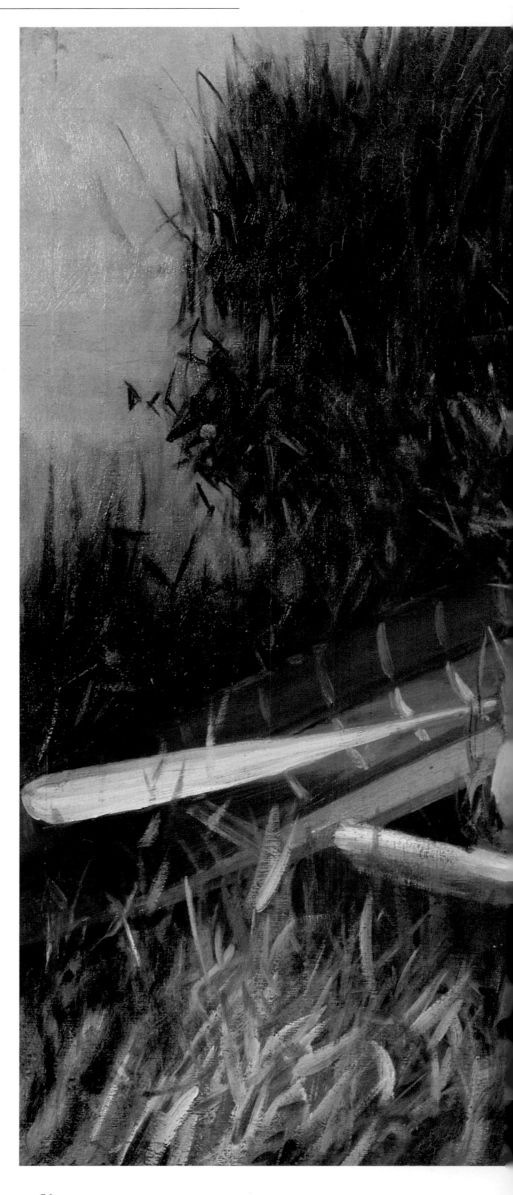

Paul Helleu Sketching with his Wife
1889, oil on canvas, 26⅛×32⅛ in.
Museum Collection Fund,
The Brooklyn Museum, NY
(20.640)

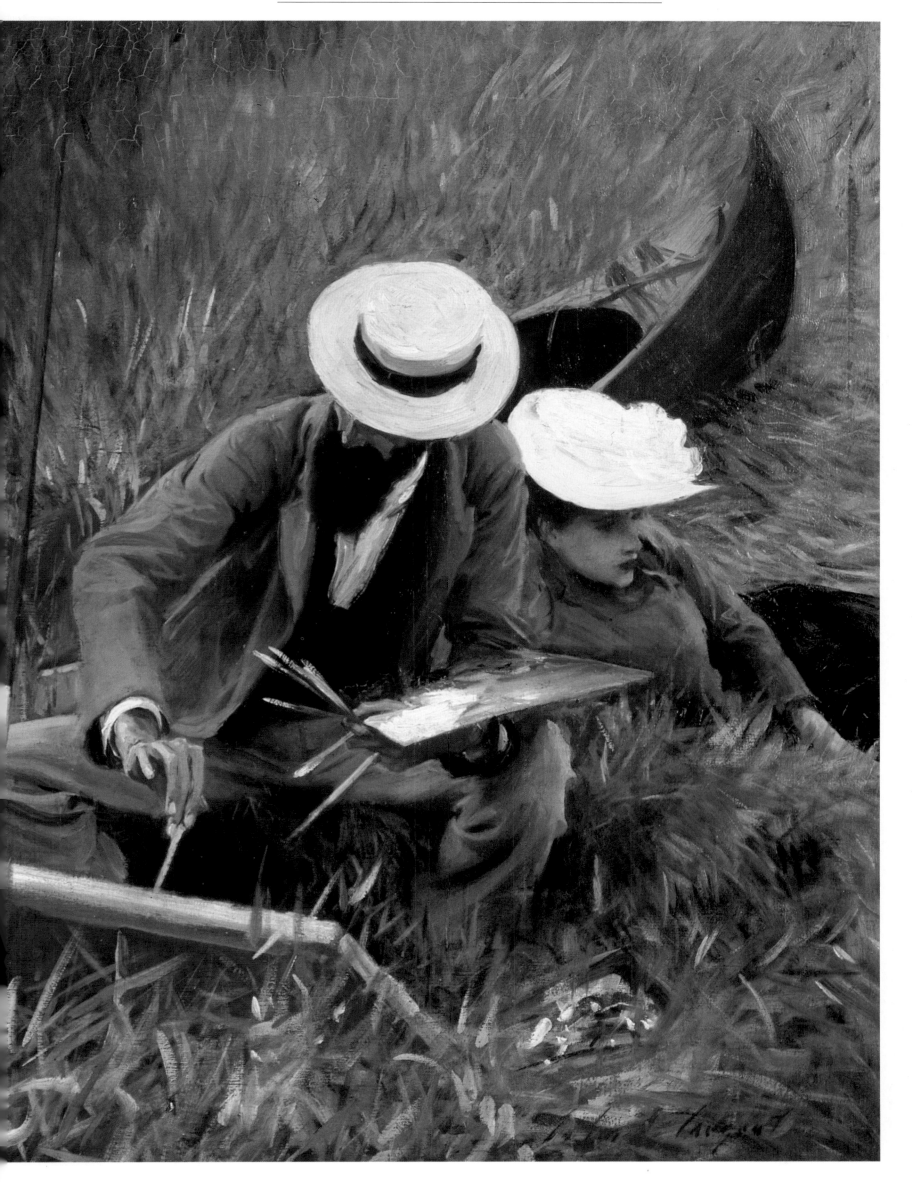

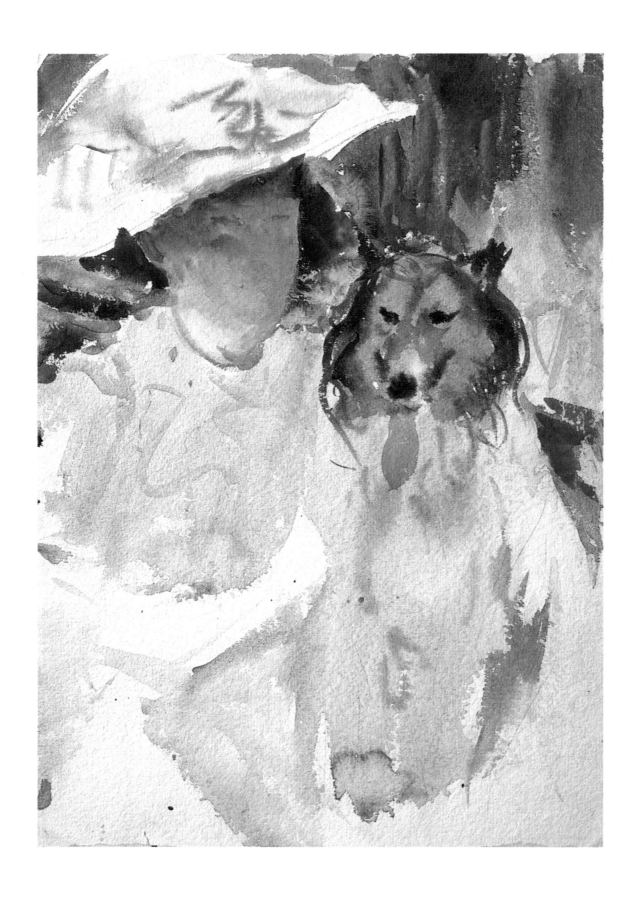

Woman with Collie
n.d., watercolor on paper, 13⅞×10 in.
Gift of Mrs. Francis Ormond, 1950,
The Metropolitan Museum of Art, New York, NY
(50.130.27)

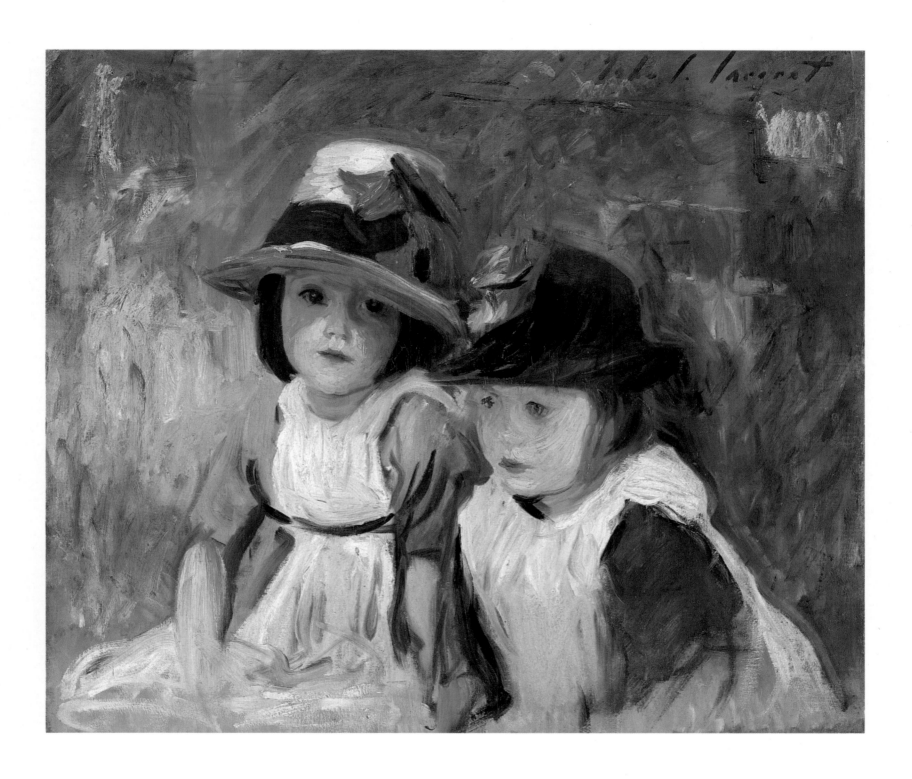

Village Children
1890, oil on canvas, 25×30 in.
The Edwin Austin Abbey Memorial Collection,
Yale University Art Gallery, New Haven, CT
(1937.4151)

Overleaf:
Artist in His Studio
c. 1903, oil on canvas, 28½×28¼ in.
Charles Henry Hayden Fund,
ⓒ *Museum of Fine Arts, Boston, MA*
(05.56)

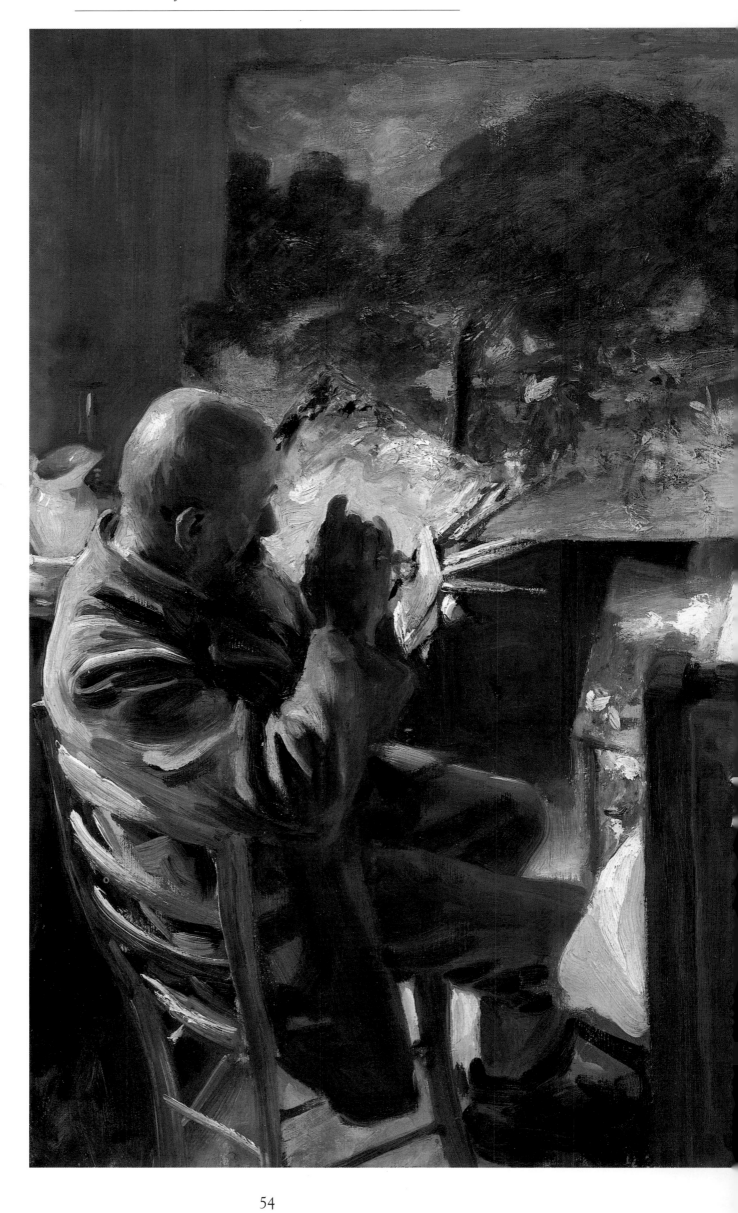

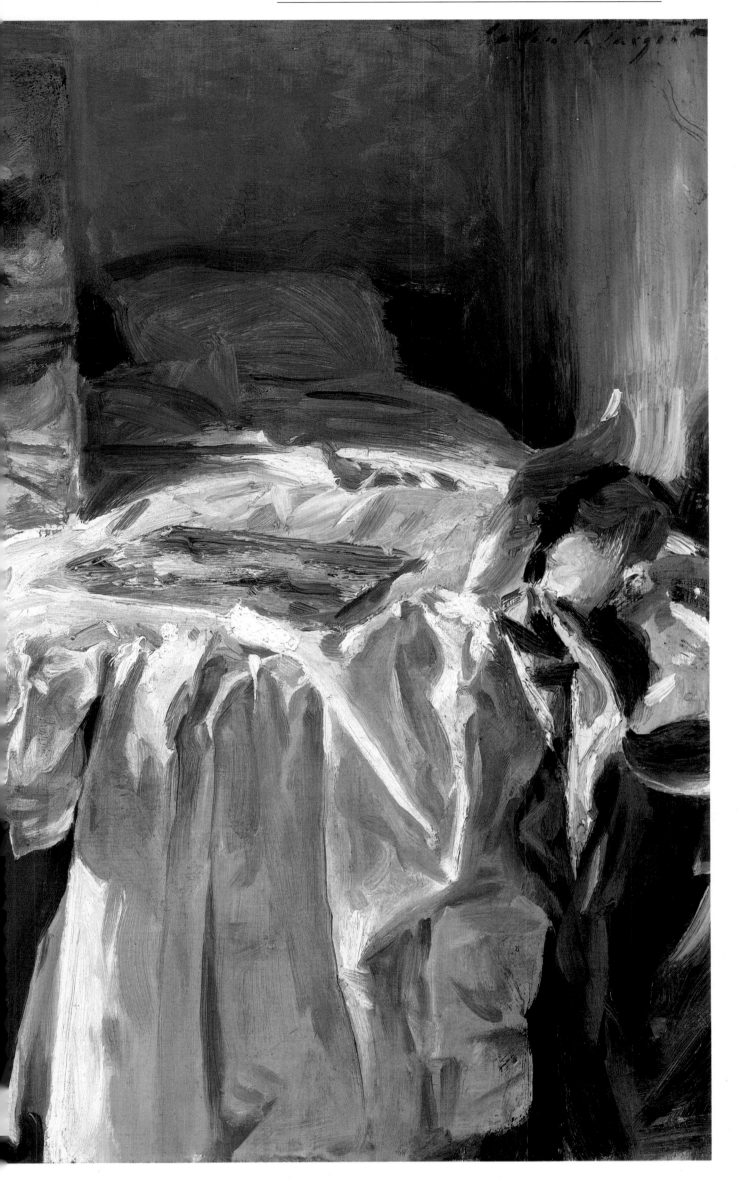

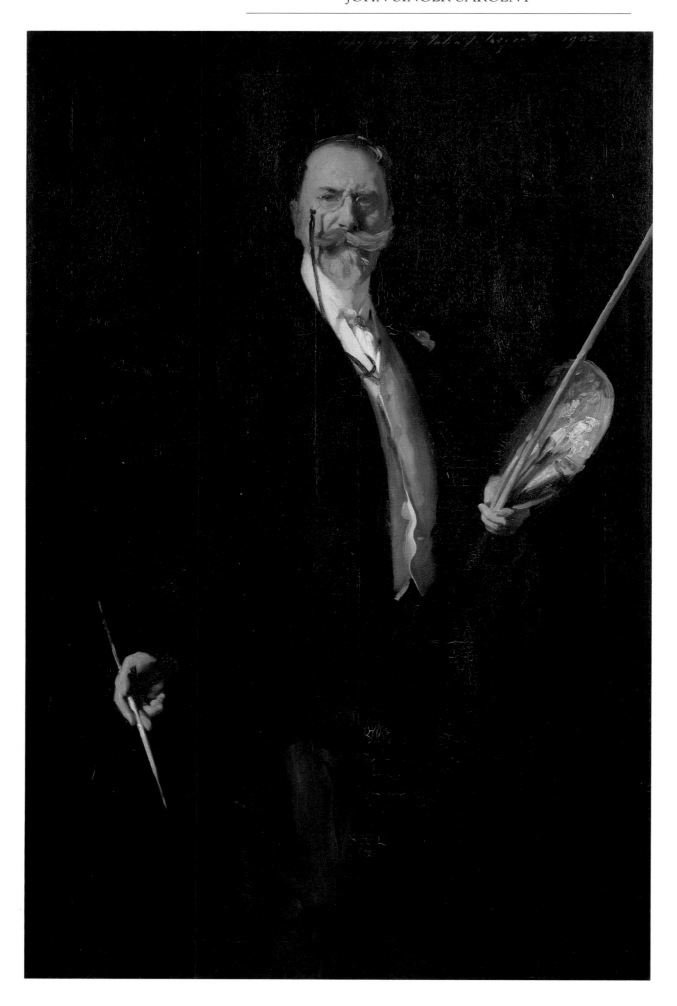

William Merritt Chase
1902, oil on canvas, 62½×41⅜ in.
Gift of pupils of William M. Chase, 1905,
The Metropolitan Museum of Art, New York, NY
(05.33)

Right:
Mr. and Mrs. Isaac Newton Phelps Stokes
1897, oil on canvas, 85¼×39¾ in.
Bequest of Edith Minturn Phelps Stokes (Mrs. I.N.), 1938,
The Metropolitan Museum of Art, New York, NY
(38.104)

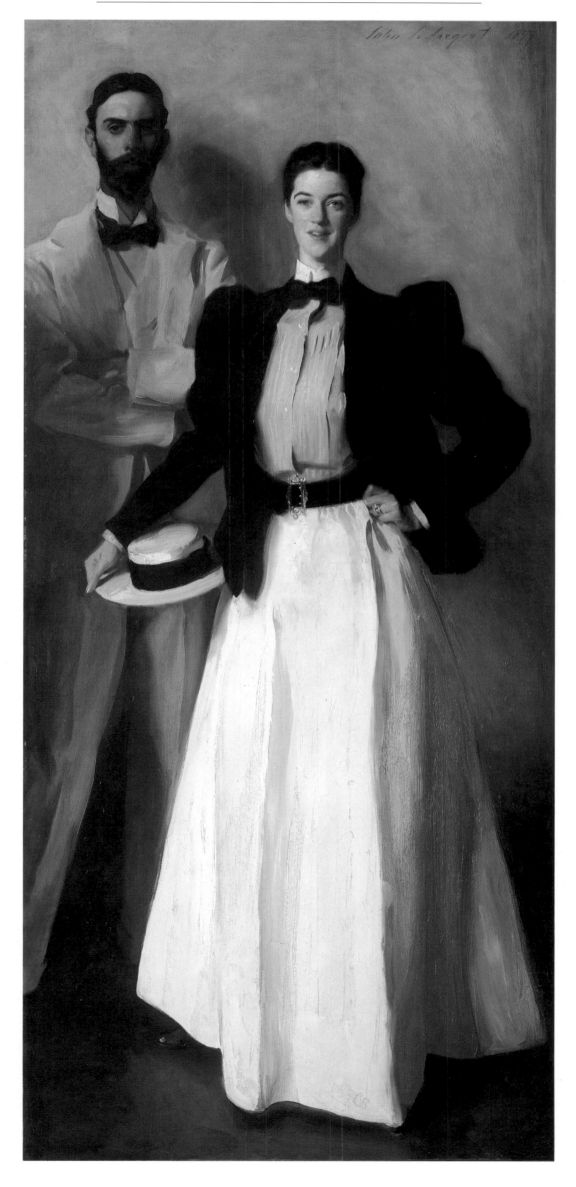

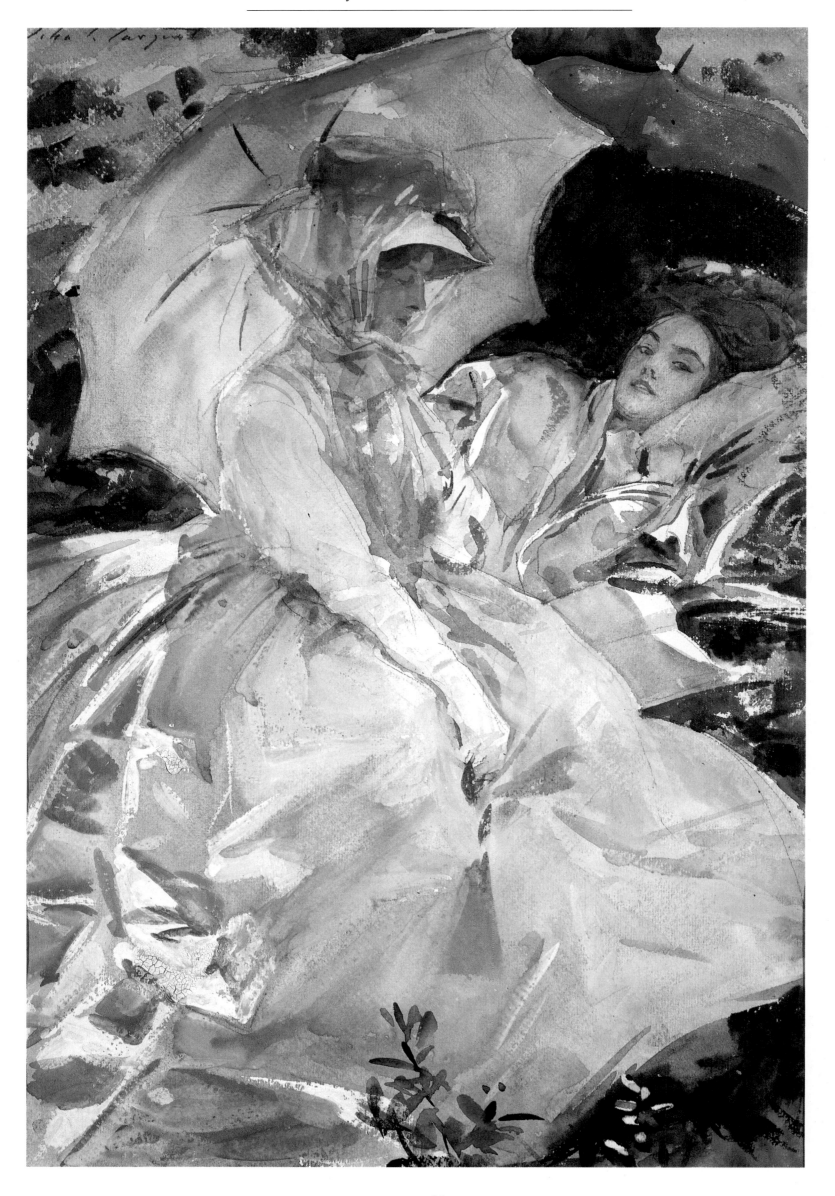

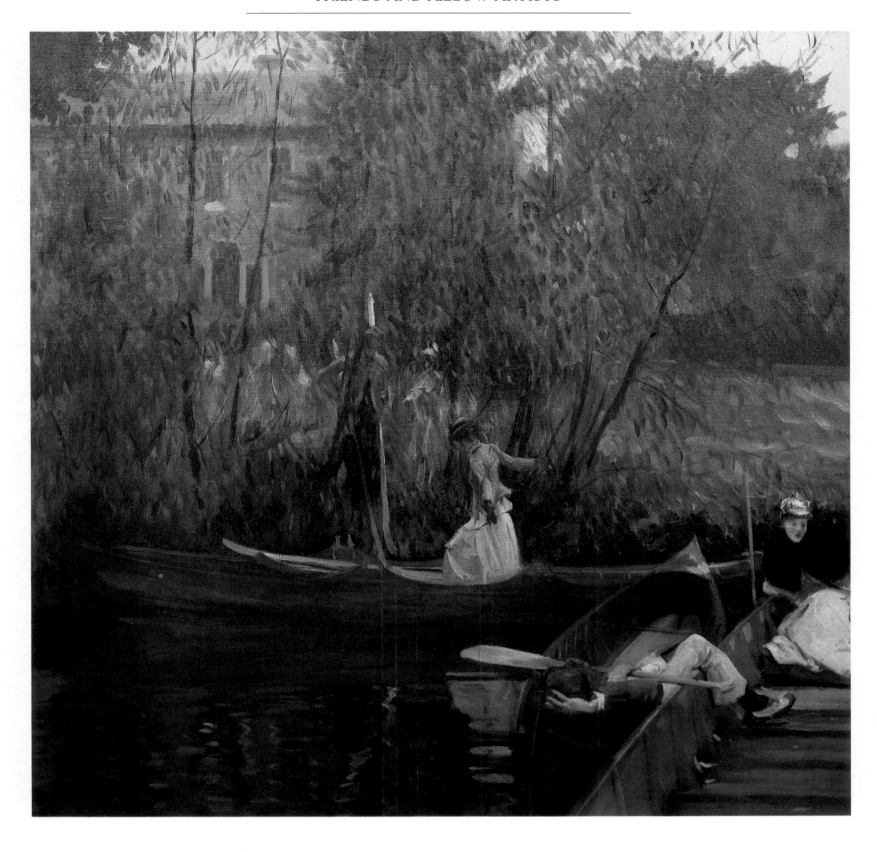

Left:
Reading
1911, watercolor on paper, 20×14 in.
Hayden Collection: Purchased, Charles Henry Hayden Fund,
© *The Museum of Fine Arts, Boston, MA*
(12.214)

A Boating Party
c. 1889, oil on canvas, 34⅝×36⅜ in.
Gift of Mrs. Houghton P. Metcalf in memory of her husband
Houghton P. Metcalf,
Museum of Art, Rhode Island School of Design, Providence.
(78.086)

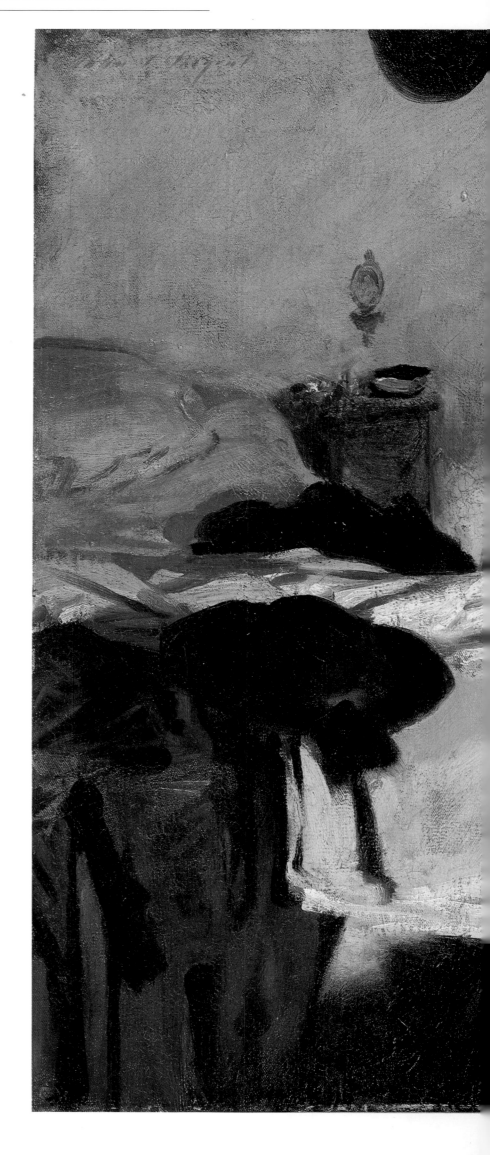

Padre Sebastiano
1904-06, oil on canvas, 22¼×28 in.
Rogers Fund, 1910,
The Metropolitan Museum of Art, New York, NY
(11.30)

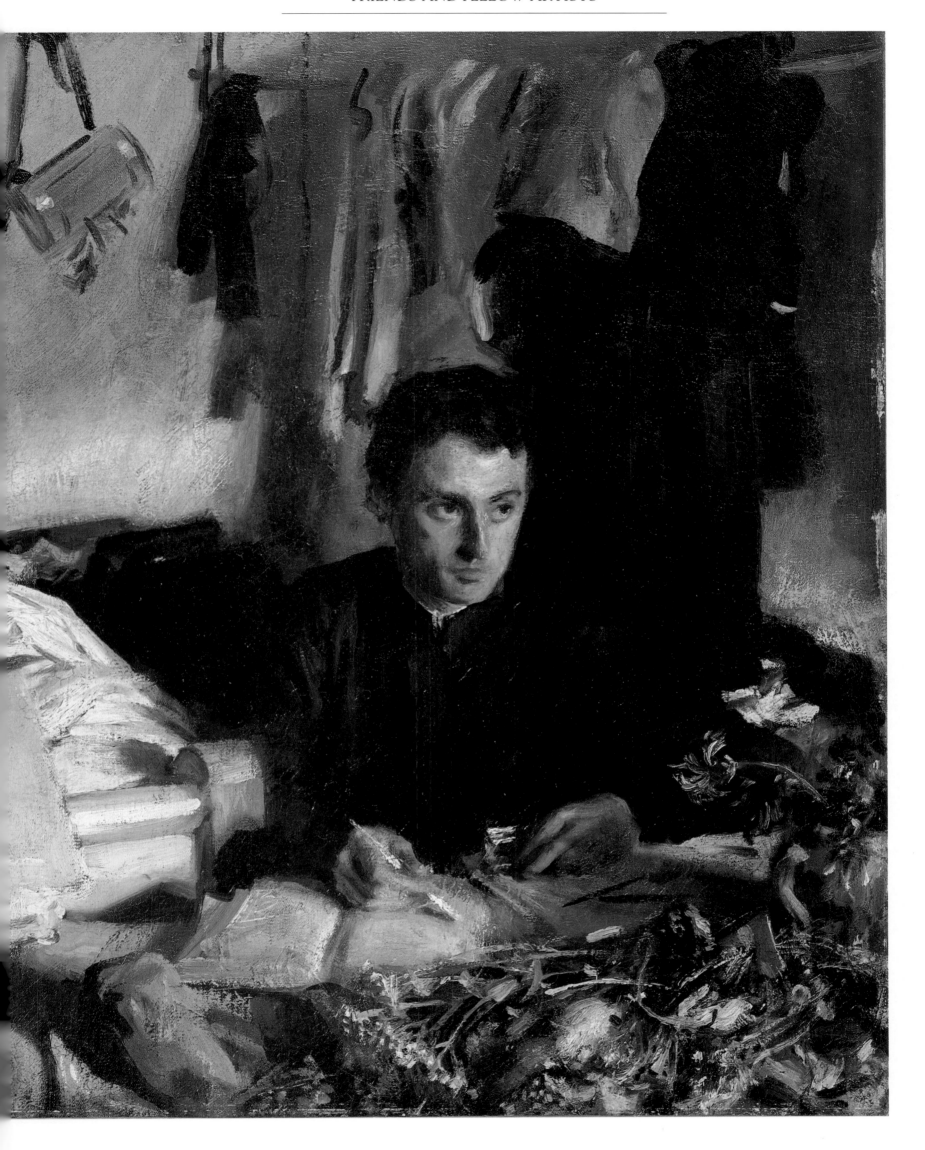

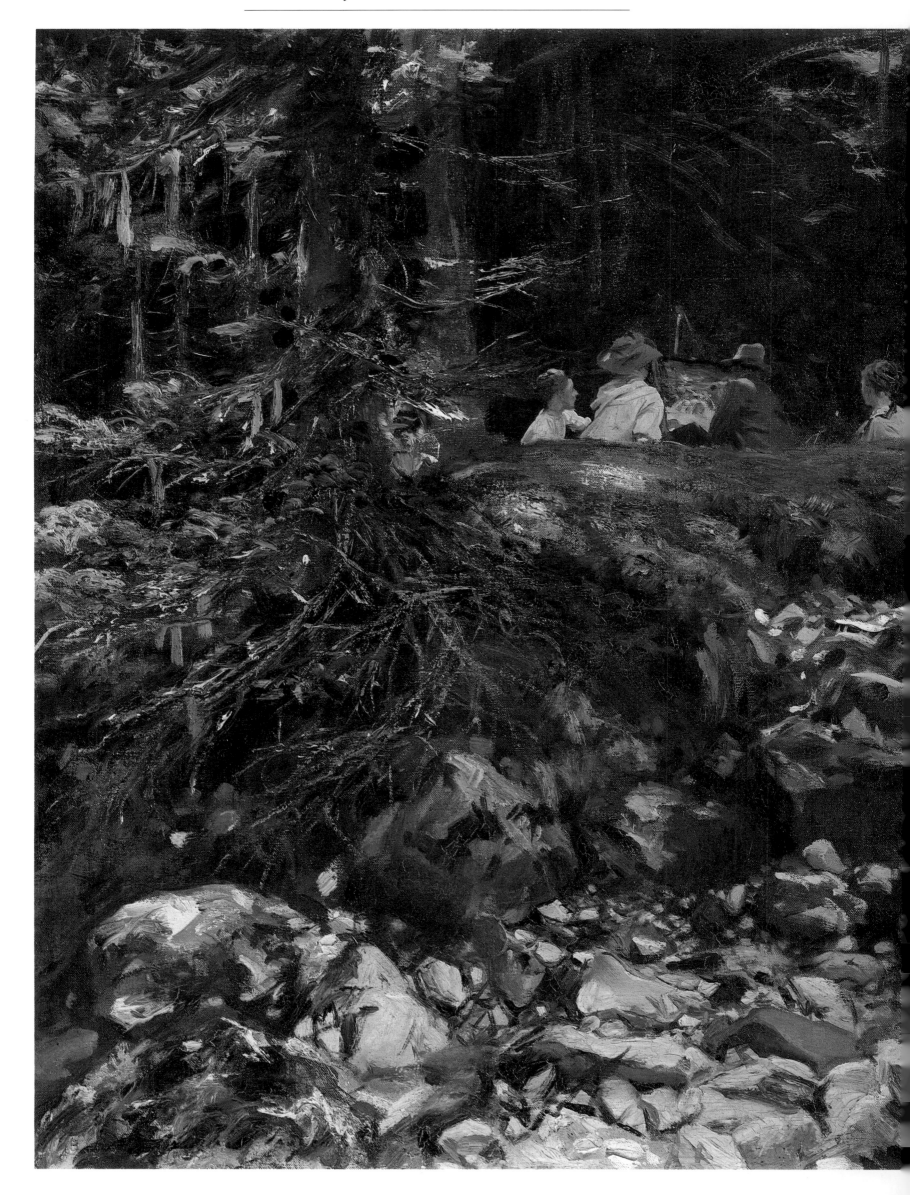

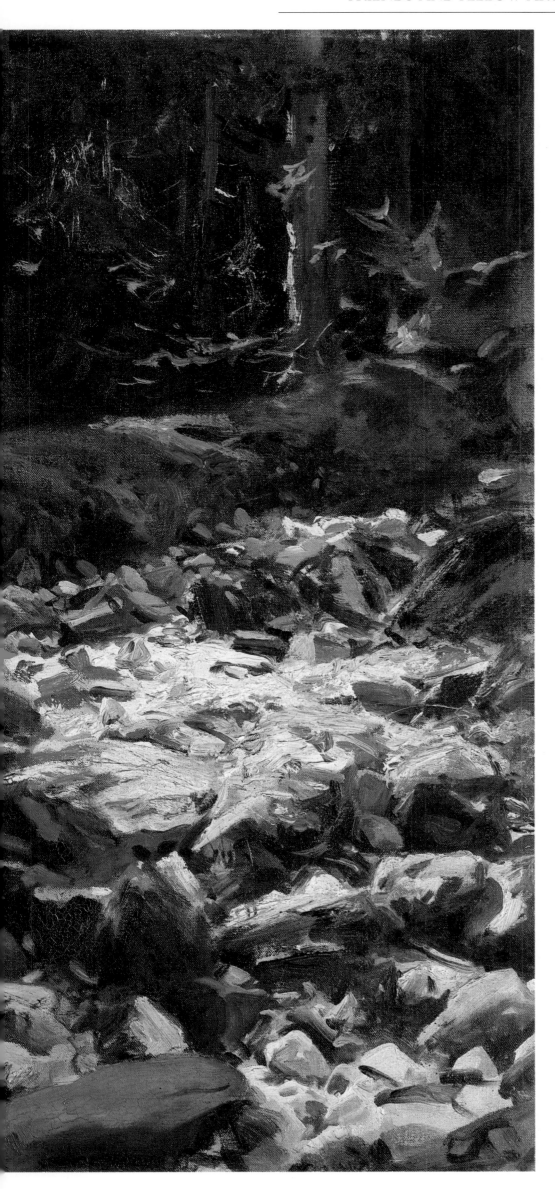

The Master and His Pupils
1914, oil on canvas, 22×28 in.
Charles Henry Hayden Fund,
© *The Museum of Fine Arts, Boston, MA*
(22.592)

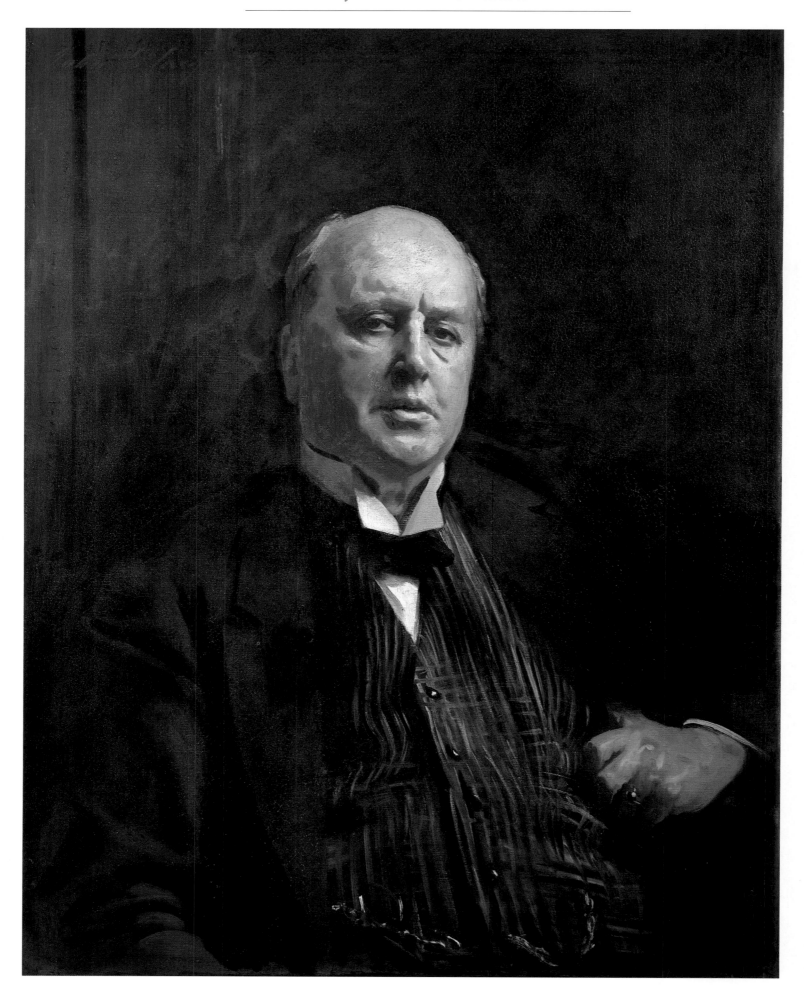

Henry James
1913, oil on canvas, 33½×26½ in.
By courtesy of the National Portrait Gallery, London.
(1767)

Right:
The Cashmere Shawl
1911, watercolor, 19¾×11¾ in.
Charles Henry Hayden Fund,
© *The Museum of Fine Arts, Boston, MA*
(12.227)

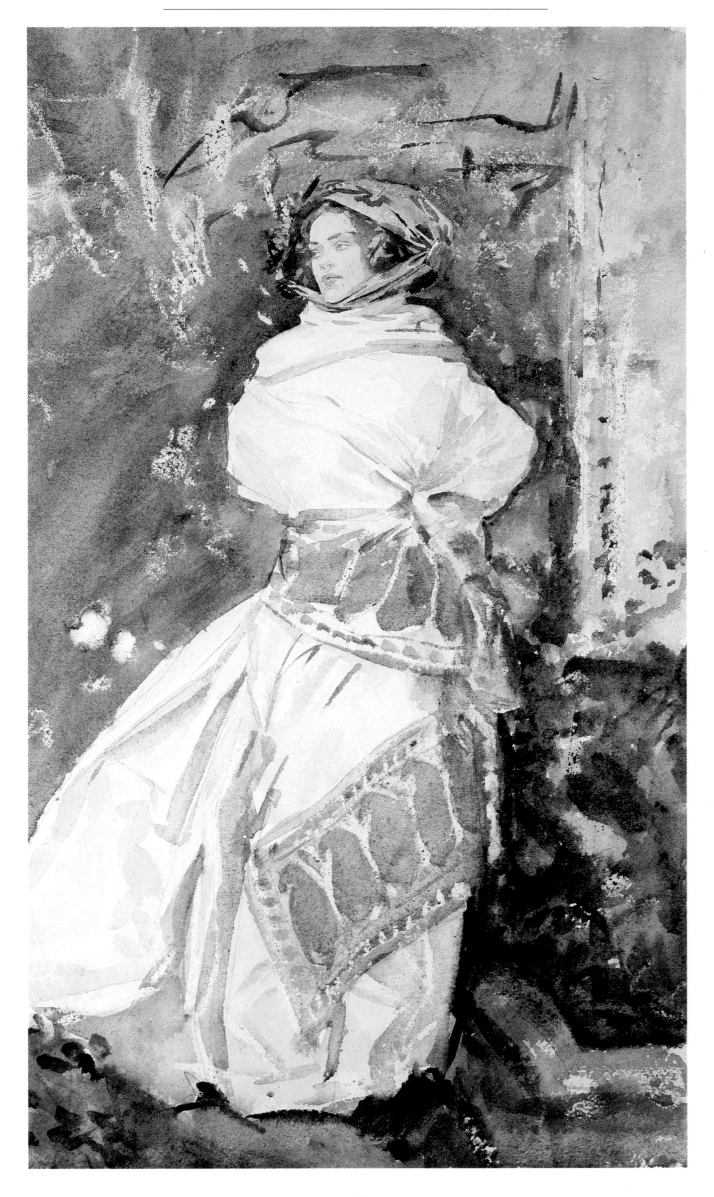

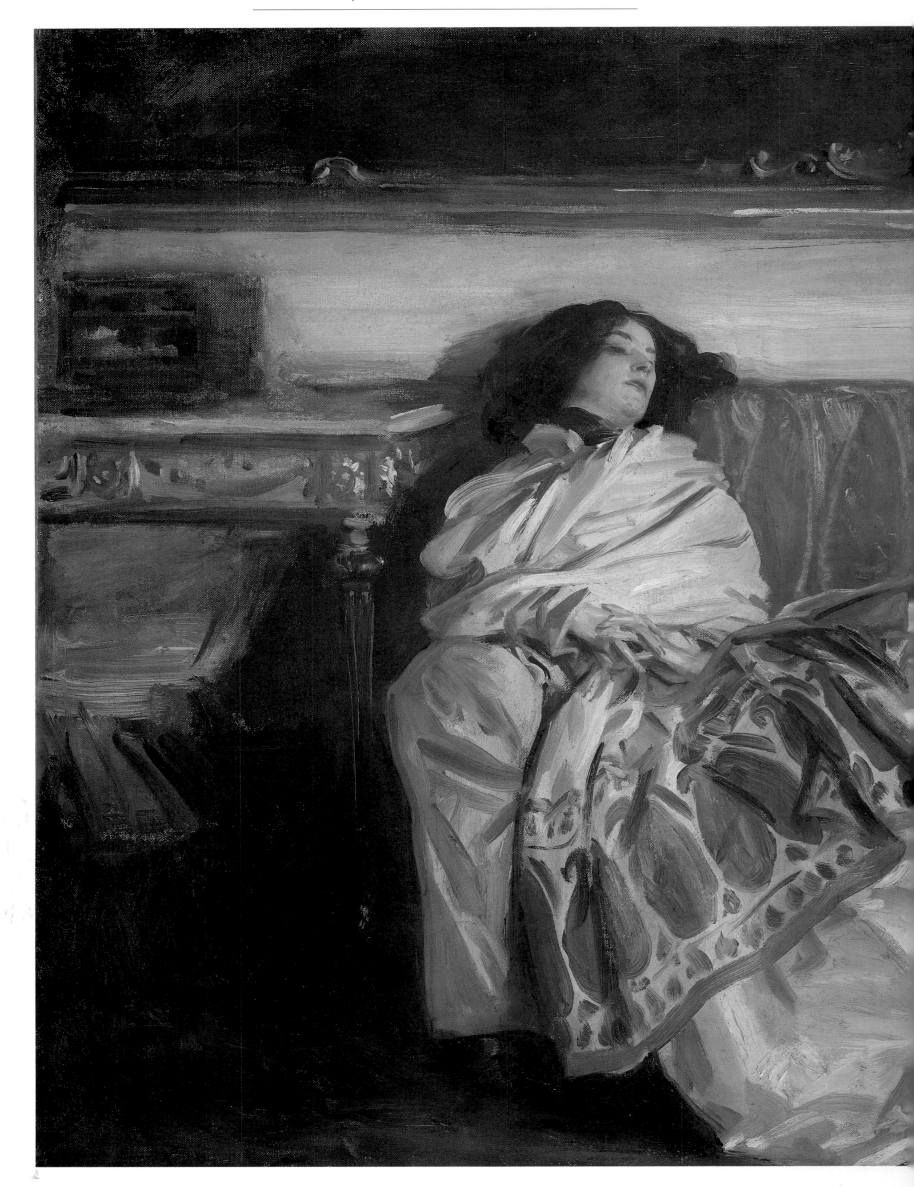

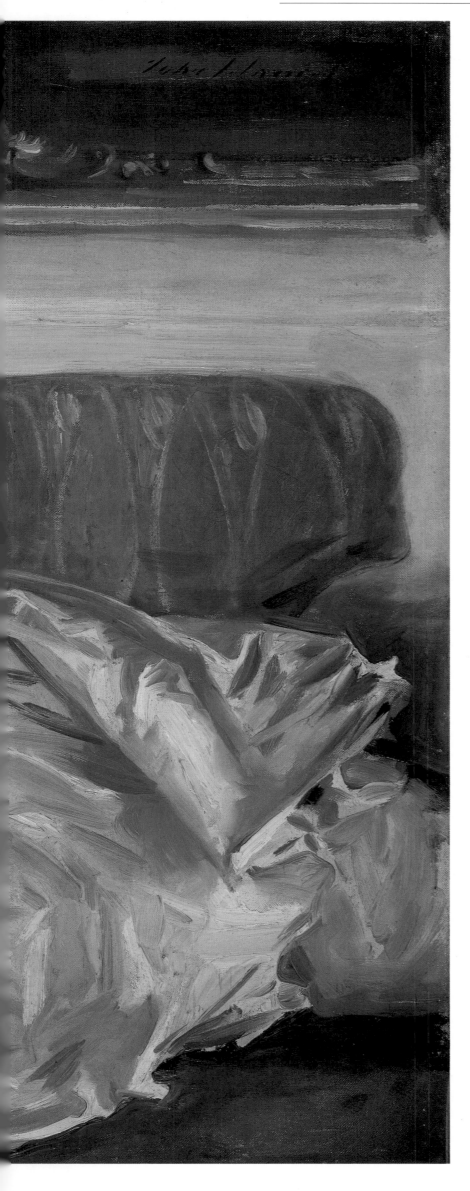

Repose
1911, oil on canvas, 25⅛×30 in.
Gift of Curt H. Reisinger,
National Gallery of Art, Washington, DC
(1948.16.1)

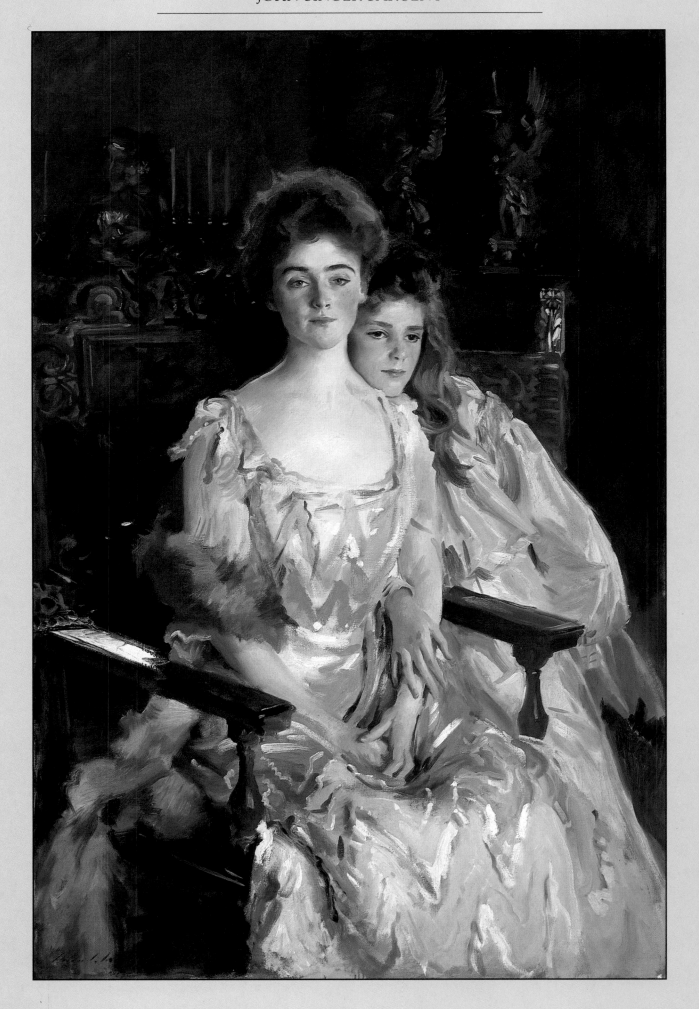

Mrs. Fiske Warren (Gretchen Osgood) and Her Daughter Rachel
1903, oil on canvas, 60×40¼ in.
Gift of Mrs. Rachel Warren Barton and the Emily L. Ainsley Fund,
© *The Museum of Fine Arts, Boston, MA*
(64.693)

SOCIETY
PORTRAITS

John Singer Sargent's extraordinary facility for portraiture provided him with many commissions from the upper echelons of London society and a comfortable style of living within the city environs. His classical training and talent ensured a steady flow of establishment figures to his flat at 31 Tite Street. These ladies and gentlemen were disinclined to have the new Impressionist techniques of the 1880s used to produce their formal portraits.

There was a certain resentment of Sargent, perhaps because of his worldly success and the renown his portraits achieved for him. These paintings did not impress several of the art critics, who were not as enthralled by these images of wealthy patrons as the subjects themselves. The English critic Roger Fry was succinct in his disapproval, dismissing Sargent's illustrious portraits with these words ". . . art applied to social requirements and social ambitions."

This particular avenue of work did not especially appeal to the artist himself, for a variety of reasons. The sitters were often fussy, demanding, and critical. Though they respected Sargent's abilities, they were inclined to offer their own suggestions for changes after the portrait was completed. To these recommendations Sargent would reply, "Old pictures ought to be left in peace."

Despite difficulties with reviewers and his own reluctance, Sargent's popularity was unabated. His friend and biographer, the Honorable Evan Charteris, wrote: ". . . during these years, it had ceased to be a question who would be painted by Sargent; the question was whom he would find time to paint."

Sargent's technique changed during this period from the Impressionist manner he employed to describe his friends and family to stronger, clearer colors, more defined forms, and the flourishes and finish required by his clients.

Mrs. Adrian Iselin was painted by Sargent in 1888 and her portrait is a sophisticated document of Sargent's finesse. Her posture is quite erect and she has a slightly puritan aspect to her demeanor. Her gaze and the positioning of her hands hold our attention – she is a woman who is used holding sway over her audience. She carries a fan and wears a formal black dress with ruffled cuffs. Her simple gold jewelry is highlighted by gold leaf and gold swags on the table where she rests her hand. Her little finger is opened slightly – Sargent often included identifying gestures of delicacy and personality, particularly posing the hands for this purpose.

A portrait of Mrs. George Swinton in 1896 is the epitome of luxury and young loveliness. She wears a satiny, pale peach-colored gown with gold-threaded trim, a tiara, and a translucent pink shawl over her shoulder. Her pose with one hand gently resting on her hip is classical. The paleness of her skin, the folds of her drapery, and her voluptuous proportions suggest a Greek statue.

In contrast to the studied appearance of Sargent's society matrons, a lovely oil of Miss Helen Sears, a young girl, in 1895 has the freshness of Renoir's paintings of children. Her expression has a softness, a questioning and vulnerable mien. The flowers and blossoms that surround her echo the shape of her hair and head, as well as the color of her dress and the bow on her tiny shoes. Miss Sears's thoughtful gaze into the distance lends the child a kind of independent intelligence as she considers the scene before her.

The Wyndham Sisters of 1899 are strategically seated so that one looks to the left, another to the right, and the central figure always looks directly at the viewer, drawing one's eye into the canvas. Their lovely, gossamer dresses look even more ethereal placed against an almost black background. The camellias in their midst imbue the painting with the scent and freshness of youth. With their long necks and ruffled white gowns, they might be swans, elegantly perched along a riverside.

Sargent grew increasingly bored with commissioned portraits by the turn of the century, objecting to the confined, staged structure this kind of painting entailed. Several of his paintings of renowned citizens, including the publisher Joseph Pulitzer and Theodore Roosevelt, were completed after this time, but Sargent required considerable persuasion.

The following remark by Sargent in 1906 sums up his sentiments: "I have now got a bomb-proof shelter into which I retire when I sniff the coming portrait or its trajectory." Yet a charitable cause could compel him to return to the easel. He donated his £10,000 fee for his 1919 portrait of President Woodrow Wilson to the British Red Cross.

After Sargent's mother's death in 1905 he was free to travel unencumbered by filial devotion and any attendant financial obligations. It was a sad time for Sargent; his mother had championed his talent for so many years. He wrote to a friend, Lady Lewis: "Everything is dreadful . . . except that her friends were good and that death itself came unsuspected and unrecognized." Yet, one senses he was also liberated.

The surfeit of portraiture subjects and the weightiness of the oil medium were now abandoned in favor of watercolors and free-spirited sketches of foreign places. Women like Isabella Stewart Gardner, one of Sargent's important patrons, would be more favorably featured in these paintings than in their stylized, formal portraits.

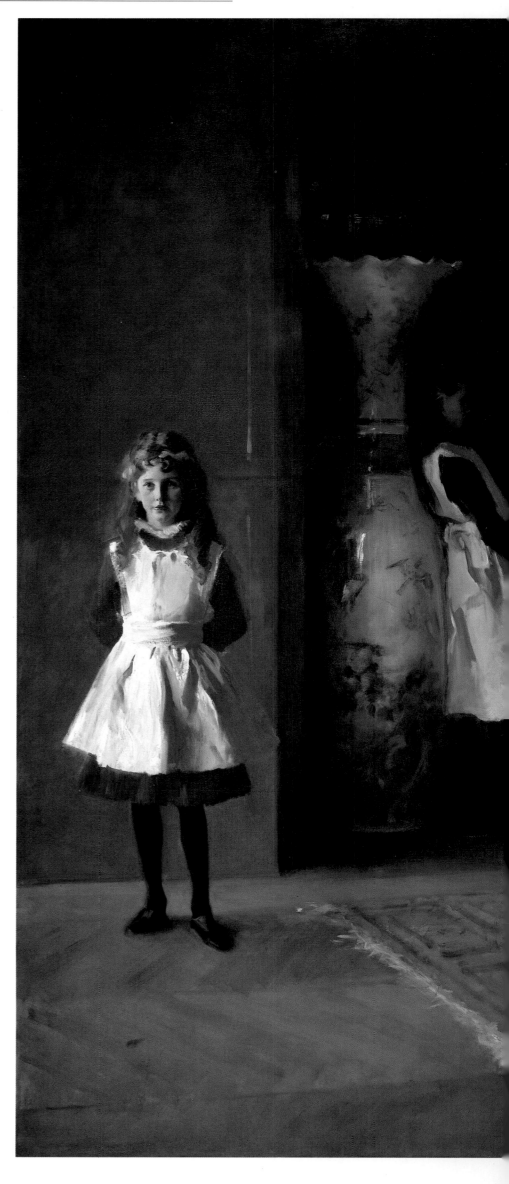

The Daughters of Edward D. Boit
1882, oil on canvas, 87×87 in.
Gift of Mary Louisa Boit, Florence D. Boit, Jane Hubbard Boit,
and Julia Overing Boit, in memory of their father, 1919,
© *The Museum of Fine Arts, Boston, MA*
(19. 124)

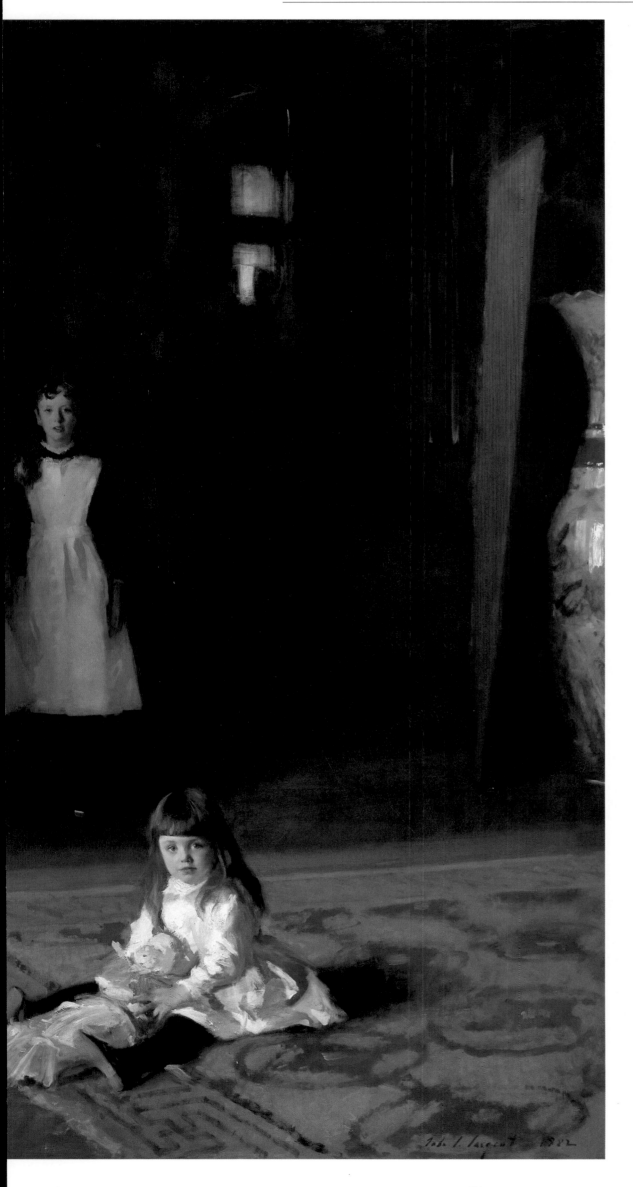

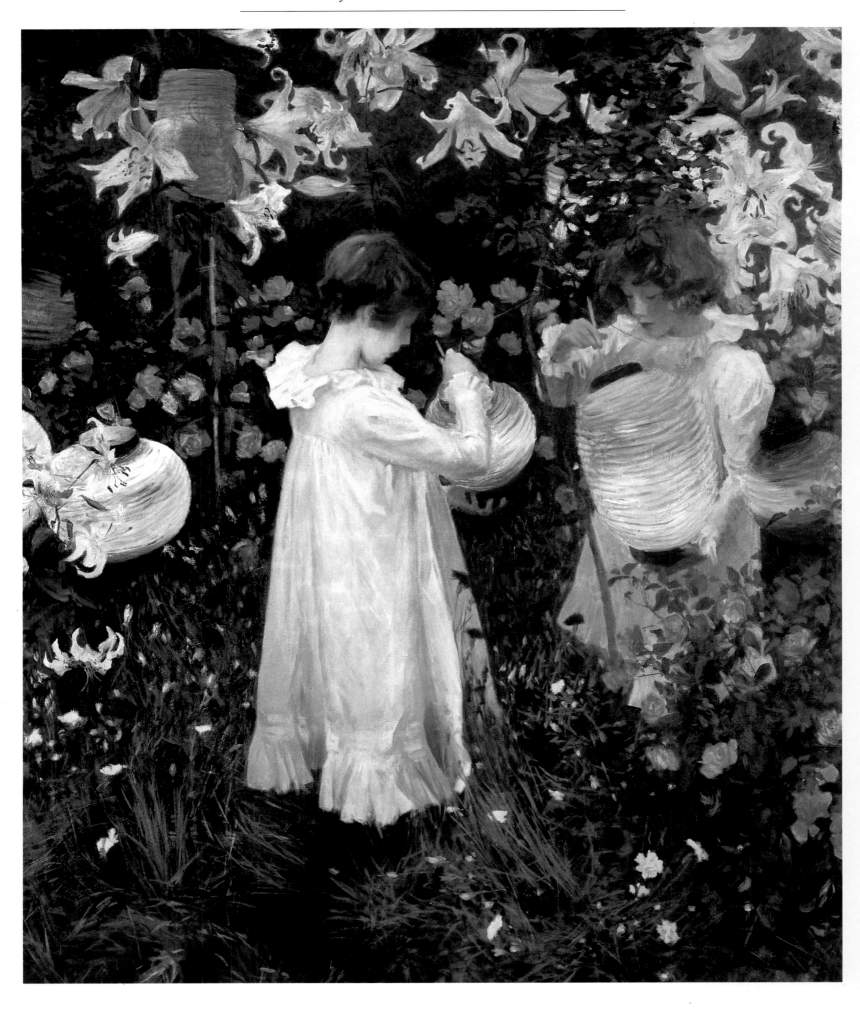

Carnation, Lily, Lily, Rose
1885-86, oil on canvas, 68½×60½ in.
The Tate Gallery, London/Art Resource, New York.
(2489P1)

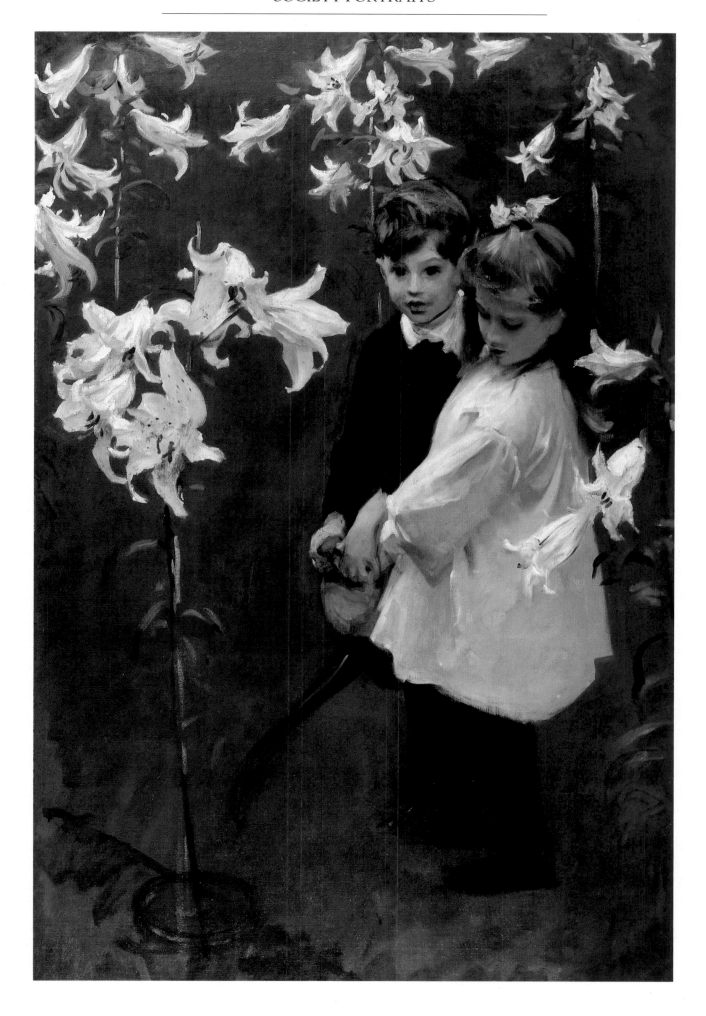

Garden Study of the Vickers Children
c. 1884, oil on canvas, 54³⁄₁₆×35⅞ in.
*Gift of the Viola E. Bray Charitable Trust,
Flint Institute of Arts, MI.*

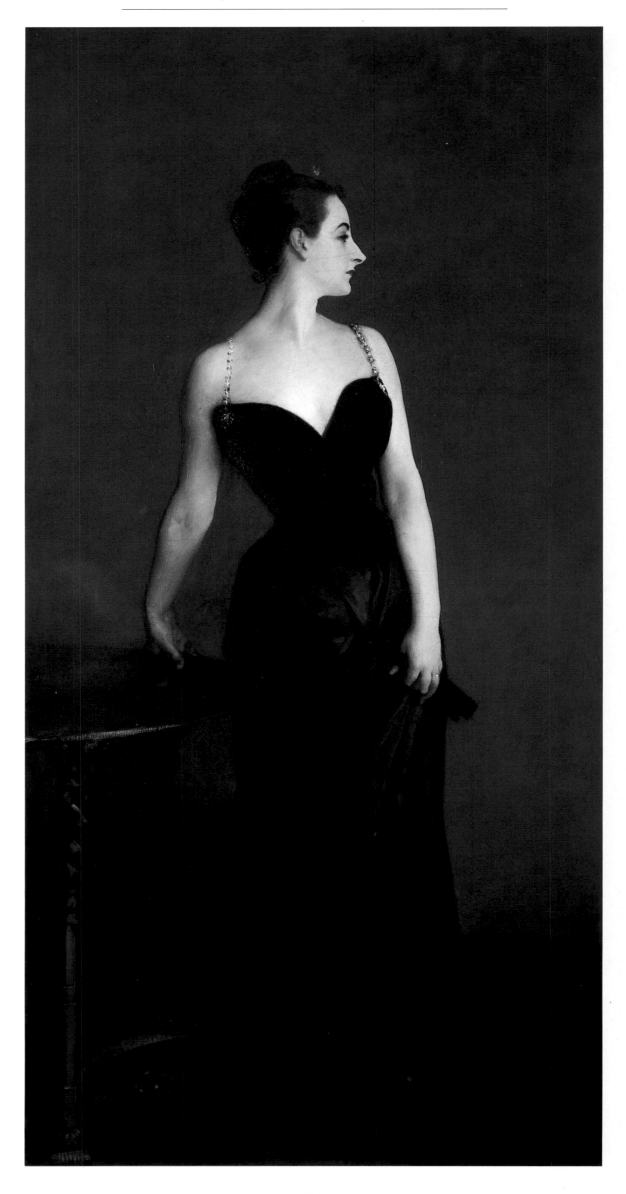

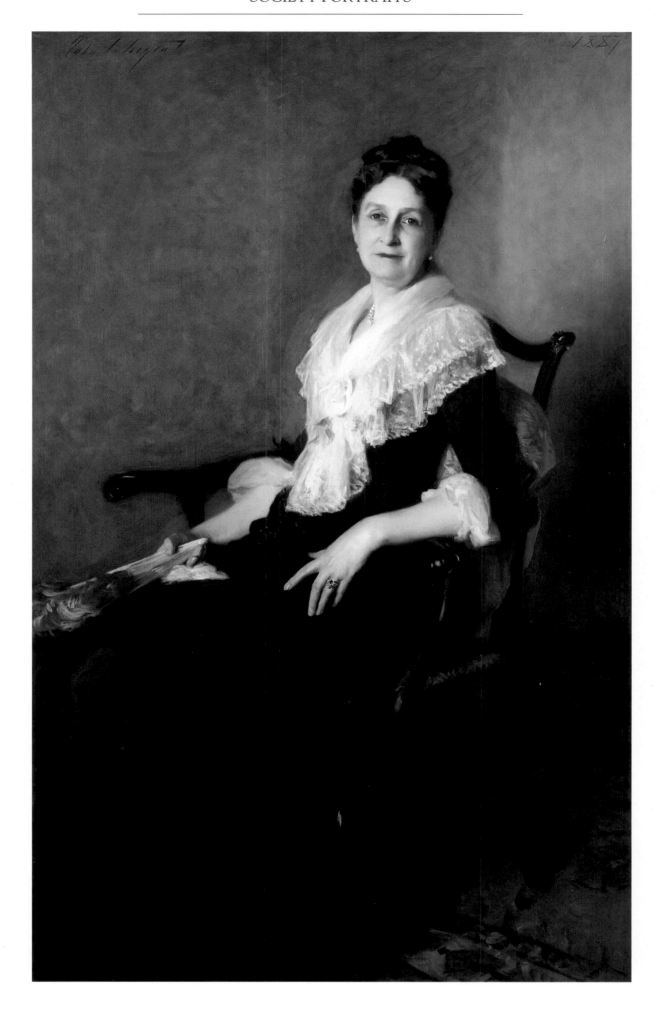

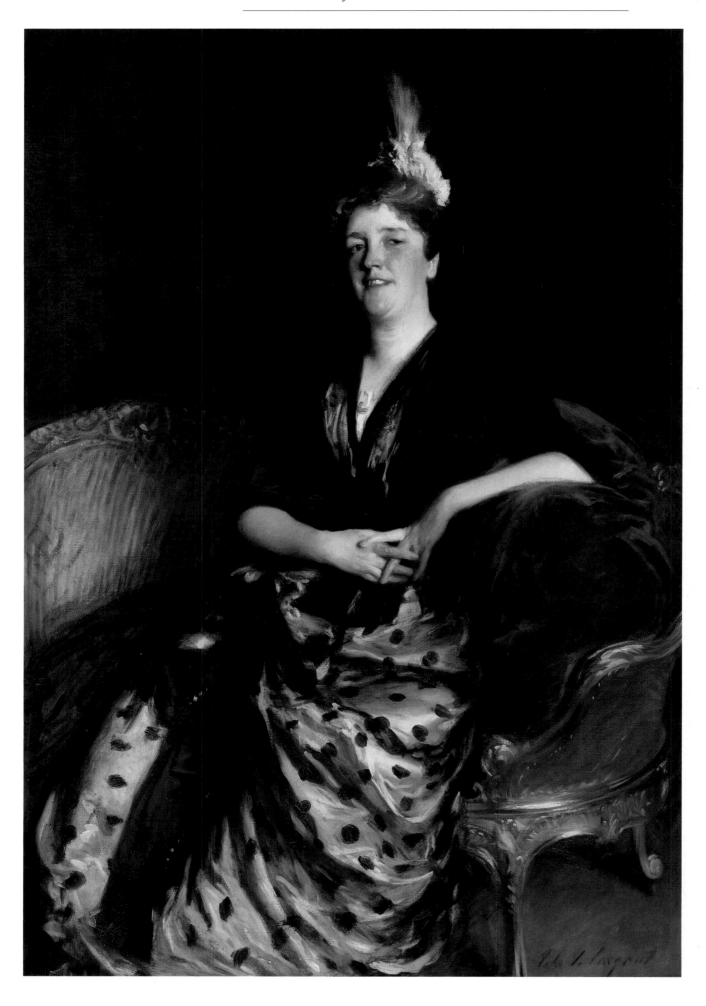

Mrs. Edward D. Boit (Mary Louisa Cushing)
1888, oil on canvas, 60¼×42 in.
Gift of Miss Julia Overing Boit,
© *Museum of Fine Arts, Boston, MA*
(63.2688)

Right:
Mrs. Henry White
1883, oil on canvas, 87×55 in.
Gift of John Campbell White,
© *Corcoran Gallery of Art, Washington, DC*
(49.4)

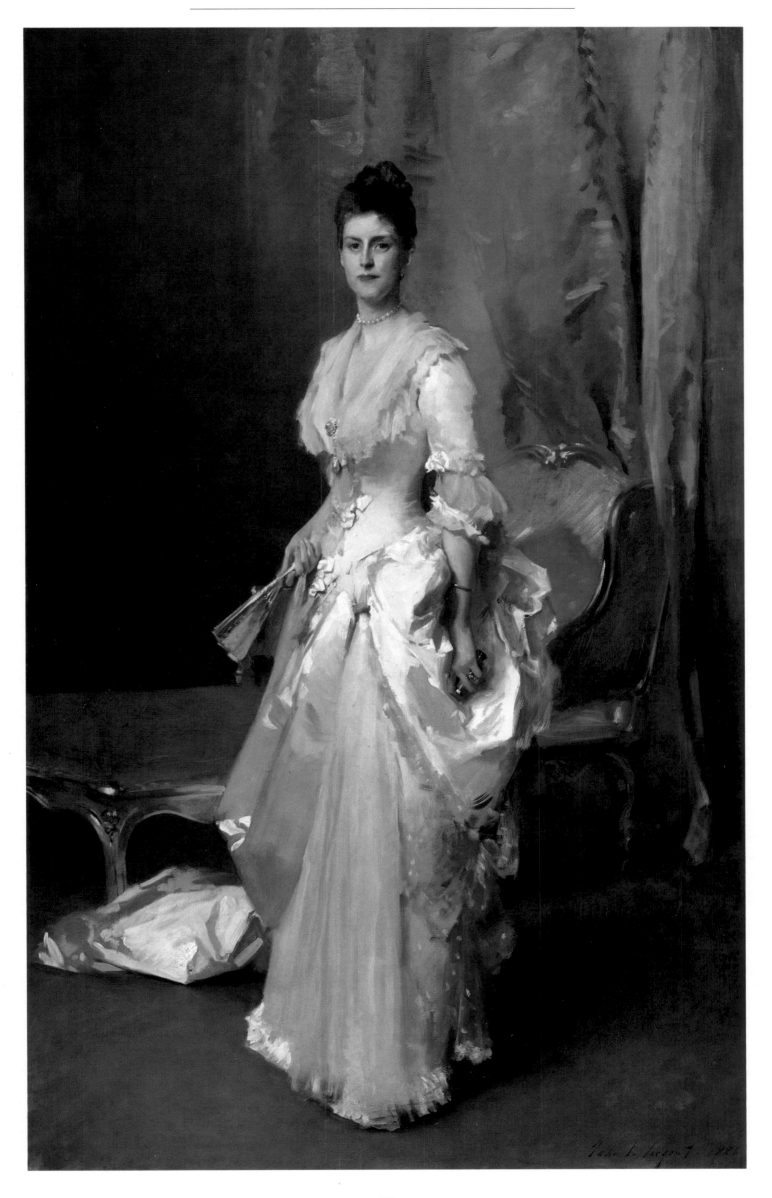

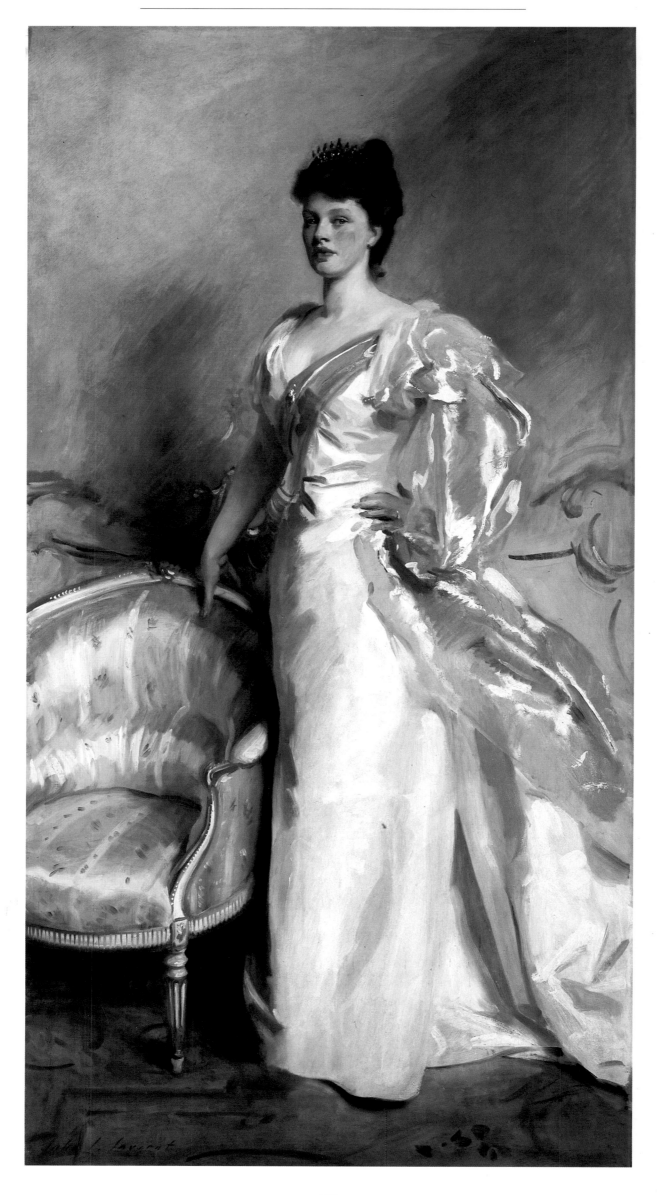

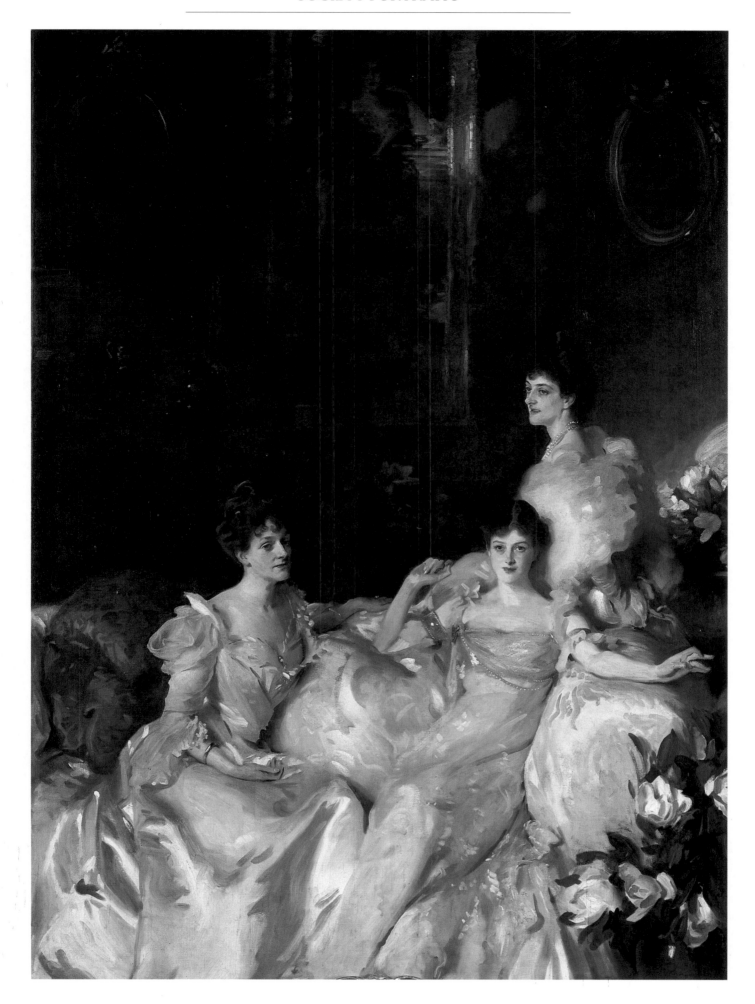

Left:
Mrs. George Swinton (neé Elsie Ebsworth)
1896, oil on canvas, 90¾×48¾ in.
Potter Palmer and Wirt D. Walker Funds,
© *1989 The Art Institute of Chicago, IL, All Rights Reserved.*
(E12479)

The Wyndham Sisters: Lady Elcho, Mrs. Adeane, and
Mrs. Tennant
1899, oil on canvas, 115×84⅛ in.
Wolfe Fund, Catharine Lorillard Wolfe Collection, 1927,
The Metropolitan Museum of Art, New York, NY
(27.67)

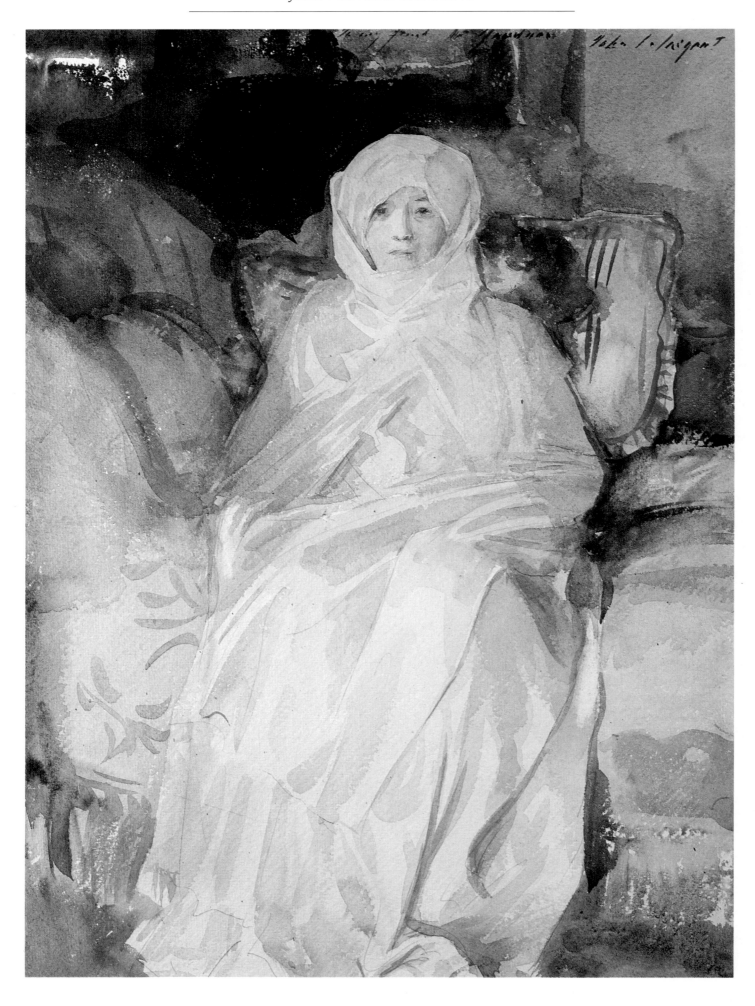

Mrs. Gardner in White
1922, watercolor on paper, 16¾×12½ in.
Isabella Stewart Gardner Museum, Boston/Art Resource, New York.
(2336P2)

Right:
Theodore Roosevelt
1903, oil on canvas, 58½×40½ in.
White House Collection, Washington, DC
© *The White House Historical Association,*
(HBJ-610-89)

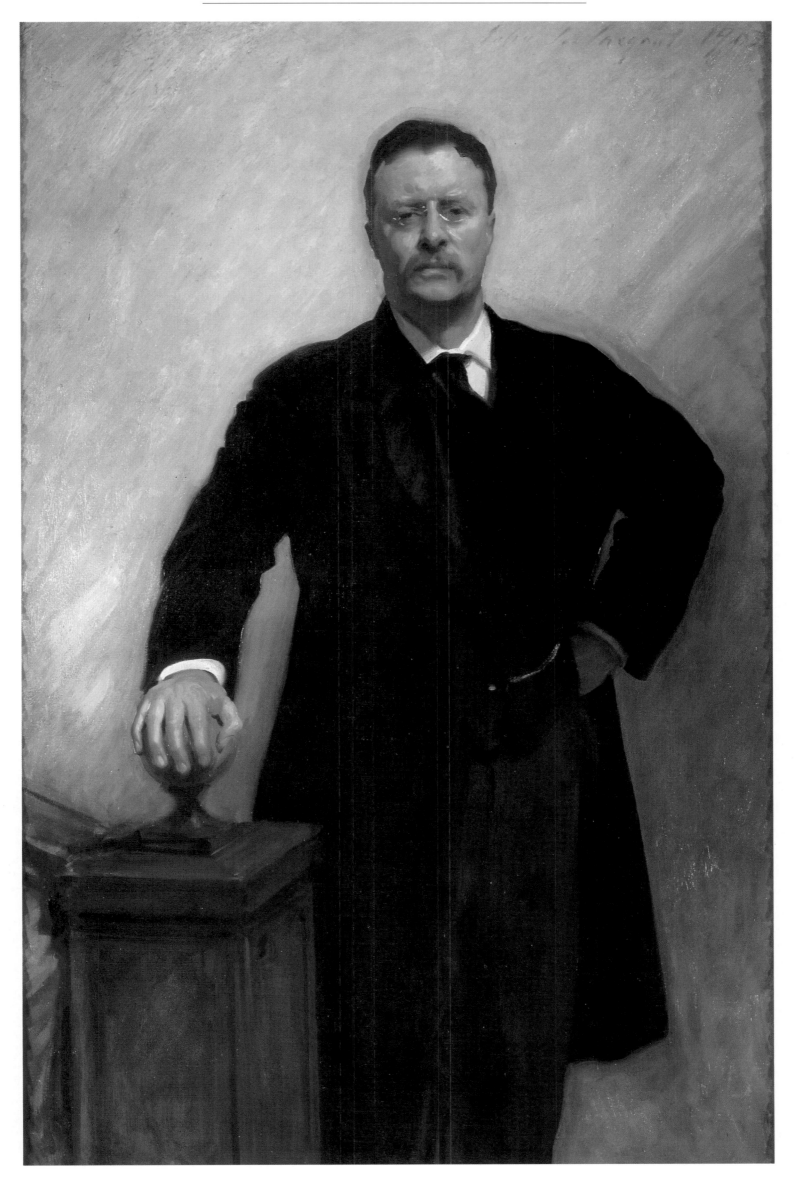

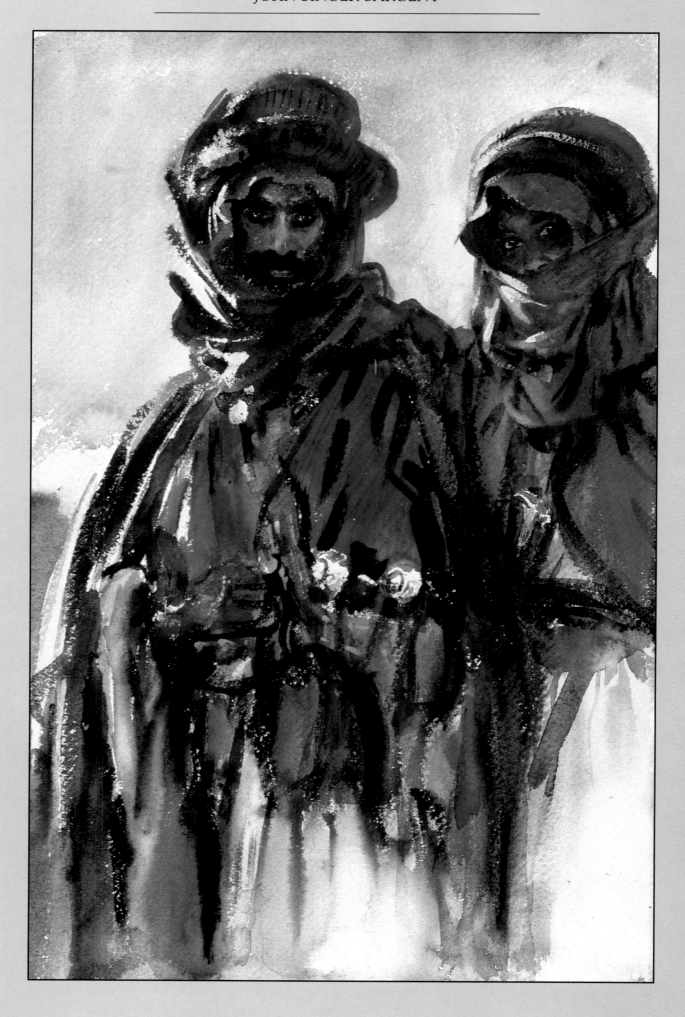

Bedouins
c. 1905-06, watercolor, 18×12 in.
Purchased by special subscription,
The Brooklyn Museum, NY
(09.814)

Overleaf:
Home Fields
c. 1885, oil on canvas, 28¾×38 in.
City of Detroit Purchase,
Founders Society, Detroit Institute of Arts, MI
(21.72)

TRAVEL AND LANDSCAPE STUDIES

From 1905 onward Sargent spent increasing periods of time travelling throughout Europe and into parts of the Middle East. He was often accompanied by his sister Emily, who also enjoyed painting watercolors. The record of Sargent's journeys, in watercolor sketches he painted for himself and at the public murals in the Boston Museum of Fine Arts, the Widener Library at Harvard, and the Boston Public Library, are testimony to a dynamic, inventive talent.

A visit to Jerusalem in 1905 inspired an exotic collection of watercolors of Bedouins, Arab stables, and green oases. The nomadic tribesmen are superbly characterized, with piercing eyes and strong physiques beneath their flowing robes. These sketches are quickly and surely painted with lively brush strokes. Sargent describes both the orange heat of the desert and the cool blue shadows cast by the Arab tents.

The casualness of these works is their forte – Sargent finds truer expressions in his people and poses for his animals when painting them at relaxed moments. In his "Arab Stable" the horses linger beside a white stucco wall while chickens scatter about at their feet. These locales look as fresh and unique to the viewer today as they must have to Sargent. They are so distinctly different from his English sitters and portraits that two separate artists might have painted them.

A portrait of "The Hermit" (Il Solatario) points out this dichotomy in Sargent's style. Here is an emaciated figure whose eyes beg for mercy, understanding, and solitude. The ribs show on his lean torso, his hair and beard are untamed, and his skin tones match the landscape. He exists in symbiotic relation to the woods around him, as gentle a part of this territory as the deer standing nearby. This painting is far from London's drawing rooms and satin gowns.

Sargent enjoyed mountain retreats and ventured frequently to the Alps and, in later years, to Lake O'Hara in the Canadian Rockies. A fisherman painted in "Trout Stream in the Tyrol" in 1914 demonstrates the ease Sargent felt in these venues. The figure is placed at the border of the canvas. His hat, coat, and boots are only distinguishable from the rocks in the riverbed by brief contour lines. Sargent's technique is decidedly impressionistic; he extends this style almost to abstraction in a later watercolor, "Figure and Pool," of 1917.

A fine example of the effervescence of Sargent's watercolors is "Mountain Fire" of 1903. Without a figure to connect the picture to ground level, everything is mist, smoke, and light. There is no hint of danger or calculated drama – simply physical data shown by sweeps of the brush. The blue hills in the distance are so changed in hue by the chemistry of the fire that the entire image floats.

In his small watercolor "In the Generalife" of 1912, Sargent portrays three women in a courtyard, one of whom is working at an easel. Their forms are so liquid they might be a reflection in a pond. Light described in pale yellow brush strokes bounces off their hats, the trees, and the patterned stone – Monet's influence comes to the fore. The friendship between the women is quickly yet effectively described. A balance and focus for Sargent's brief notations is achieved in the placement of this triad.

On a visit to the United States in 1911 Sargent had occasion to go to Florida. His watercolor sketch "Palmettos" is very close in style to Winslow Homer's watercolors on similar themes from this era. The kinship between the two artists is most apparent in their watercolor landscapes and studies of resort and vacation scenes. Sargent's classical European training enabled him to paint society figures with unparalleled finesse. Homer's familiarity with the sea and the isolation on the Maine coast, as well as his rugged, self-taught techniques, produced unmatched marine canvases.

"Bringing Down Marble from the Quarries to Carrara" displays Sargent's mastery of perspective and superb sense of scale. In the finished oil painting the men at work are small in comparison to the massive quarries, yet their gestures convey the hard physical labor and skill required by their occupation. The long, lean rope lines devised to transport the rock are placed diagonally across the canvas. The viewer's eye follows them back to their source and feels the tension in their pull. Except for a small patch of blue sky that accentuates the monochromatic vista and a bright red kerchief worn by the stoneworker in the foreground, the entire landscape is pale ochre, maize, and tan, with flecks of purple shadow.

Sargent maintained a Spartan regimen and stayed in a simple hut when he was at Carrara. His pictures tell of a way of life far removed from the rarefied air of London society. Yet the years of objectively proportioning and delineating faces, features, and forms were now applied to the vast, unpopulated regions of the world he visited.

Sargent's paintings of the waterfalls and camp scenes in the Canadian Rockies in 1916 are also reminiscent of the grandeur in Winslow Homer's work. They are excellent examples of Sargent's ability to paint light. The tents are translucent white and the cascading mist of "Yoho Falls" has an opaline beauty. The natural world renewed and rekindled Sargent and he communicated his keen perceptions of it in paintings like these.

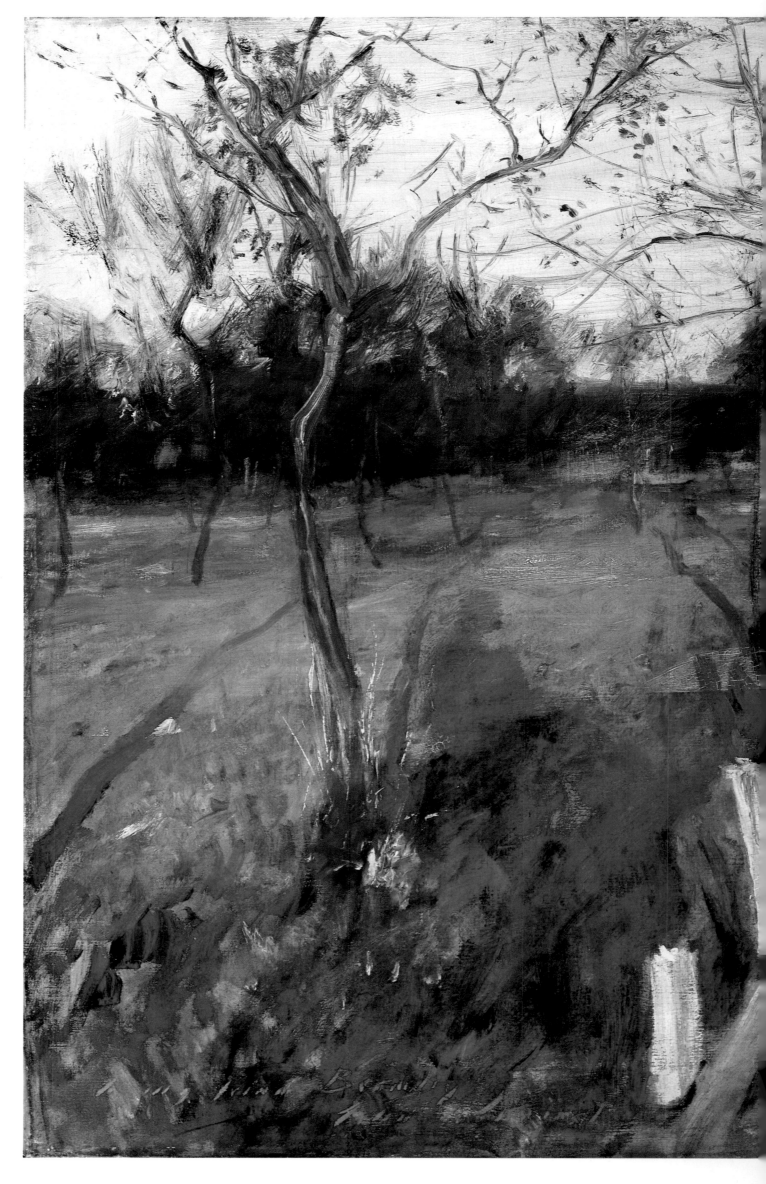

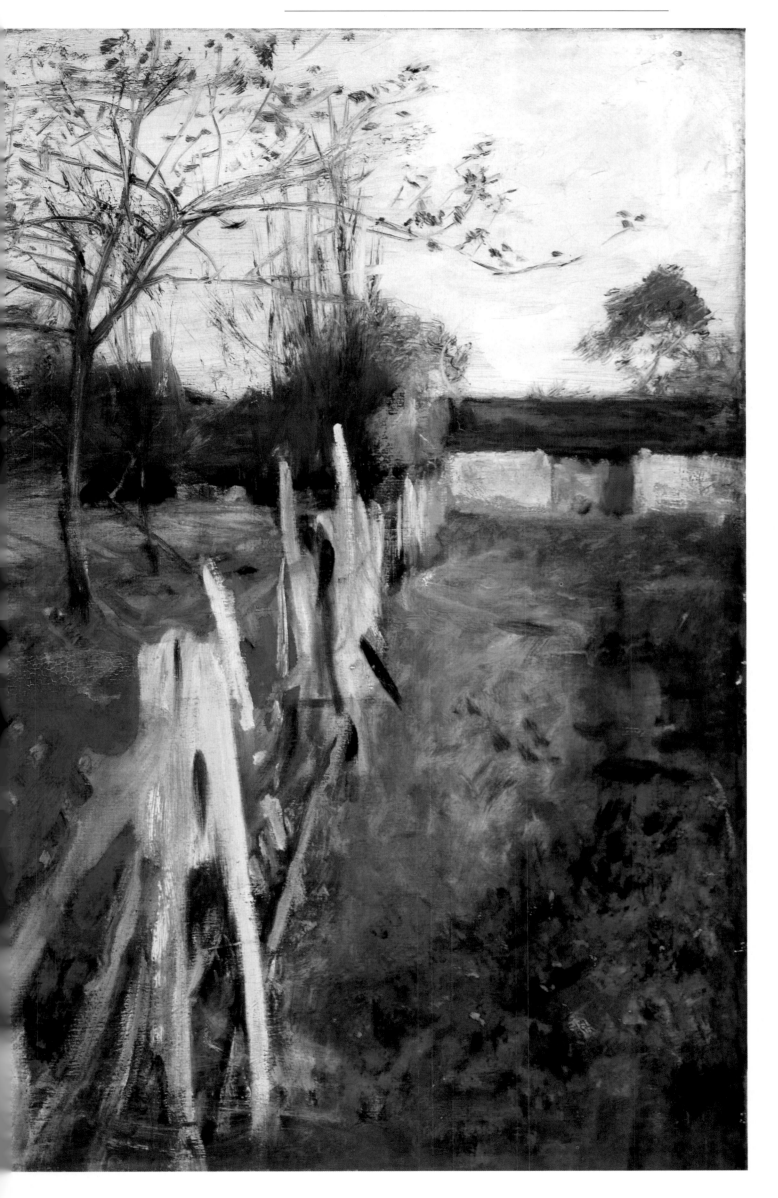

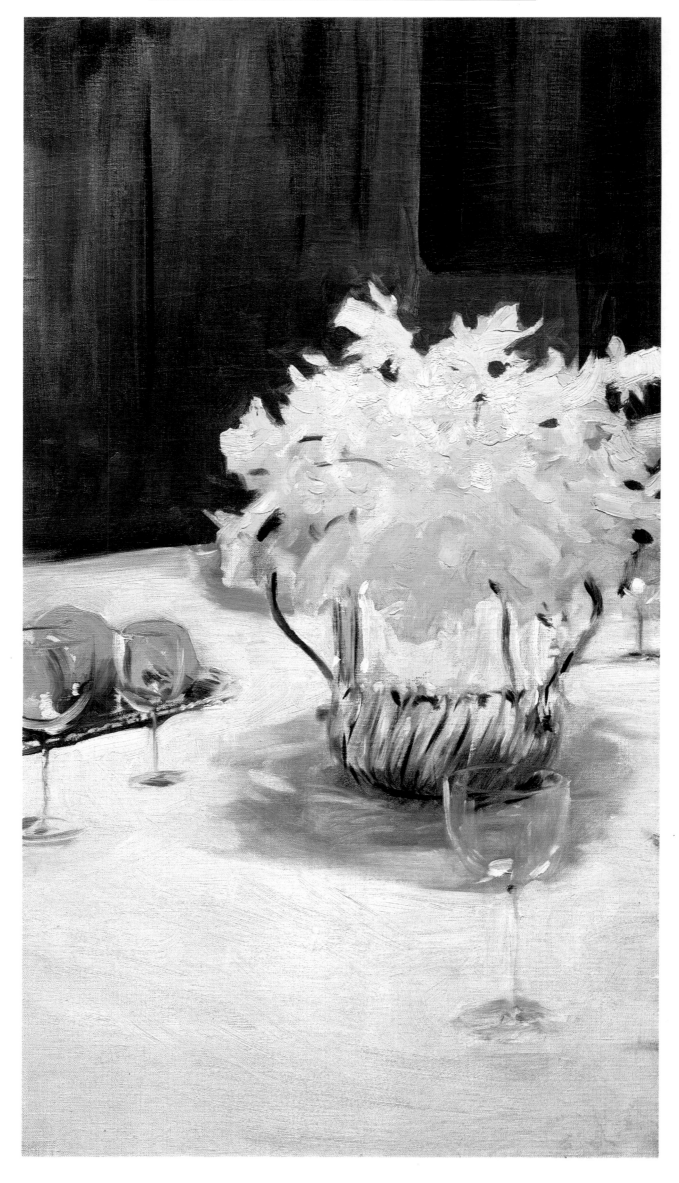

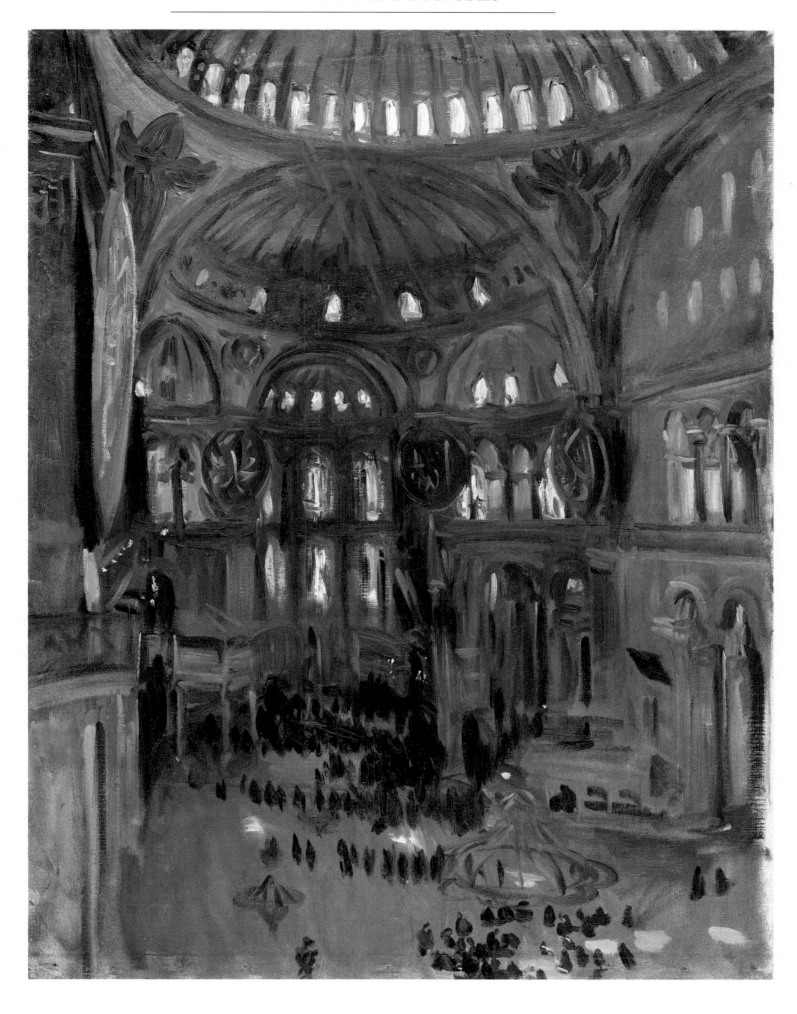

Left:
Still Life with Daffodils
n.d., oil on canvas, 32×18 in.
Edwin Austin Abbey Memorial Collection,
Yale University Art Gallery, New Haven, CT
(1937.2556)

Sketch of Santa Sofia
c. 1891, oil on canvas, 31½×24¼ in.
Gift of Mrs. Francis Ormond, 1950,
The Metropolitan Museum of Art, New York, NY
(50.13C.18)

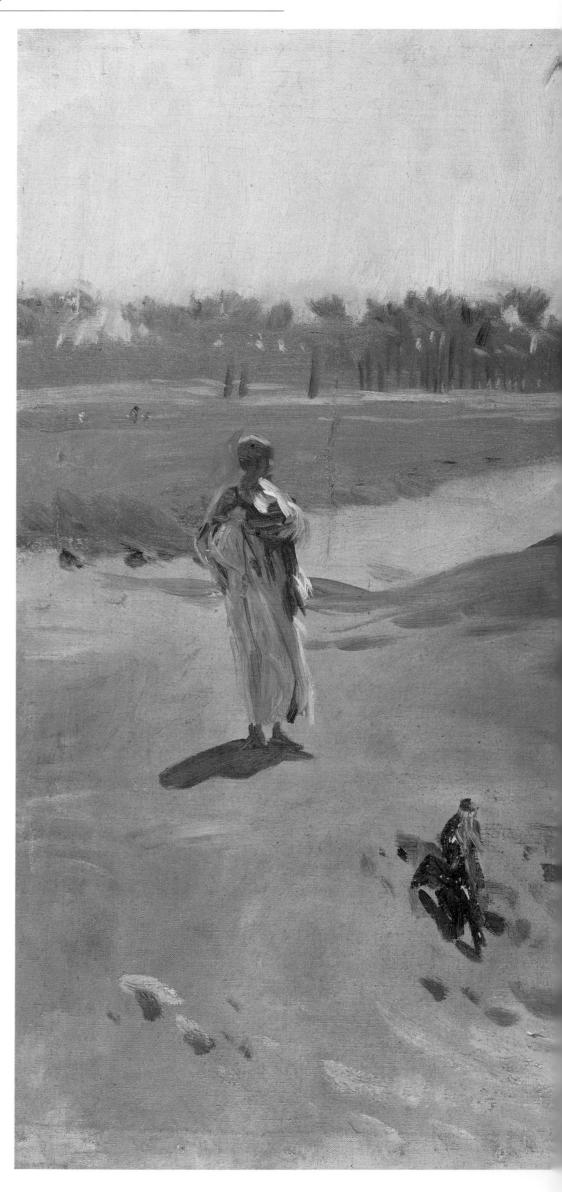

Landscape with Goatherd
1905, oil on canvas, 24¼×31⅞ in.
Gift of Mrs. Francis Ormond, 1950,
The Metropolitan Museum of Art, New York, NY
(50.130.17)

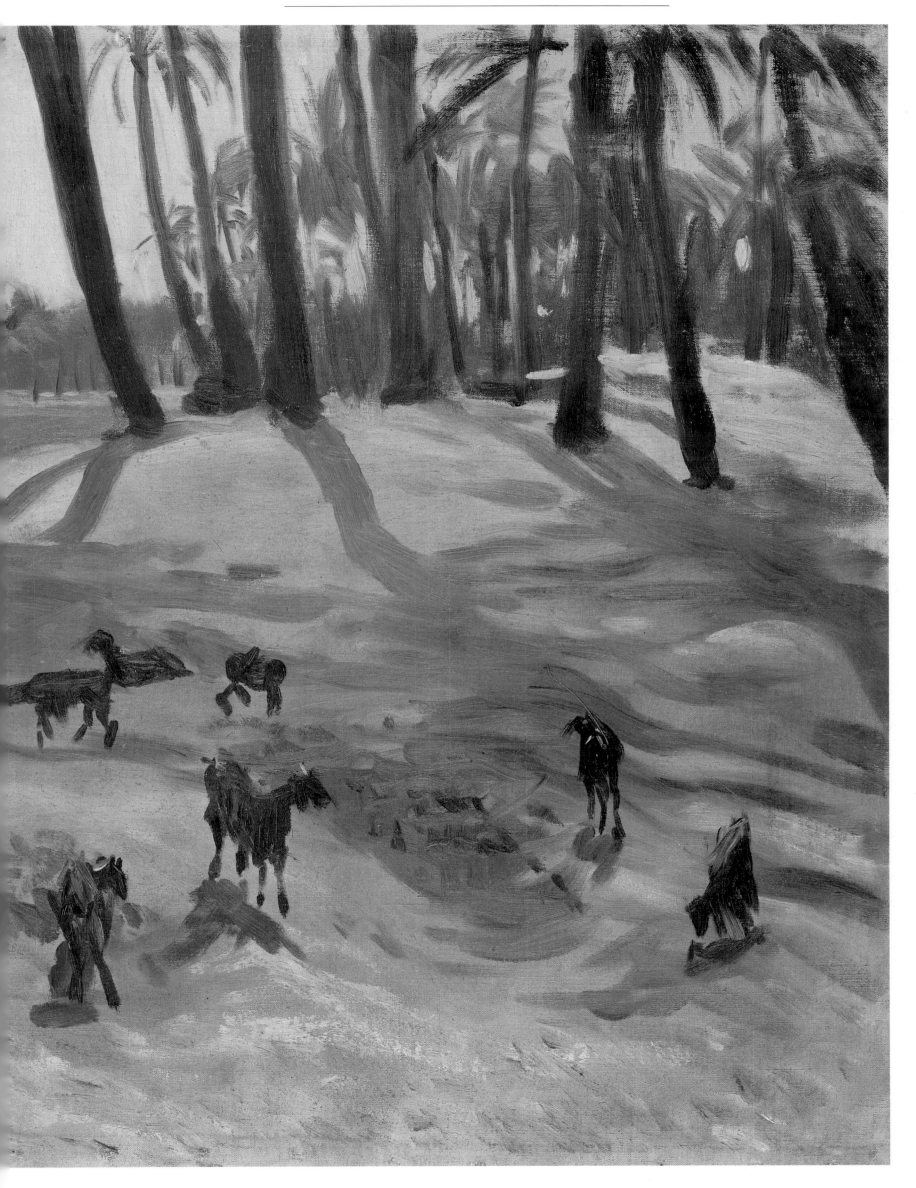

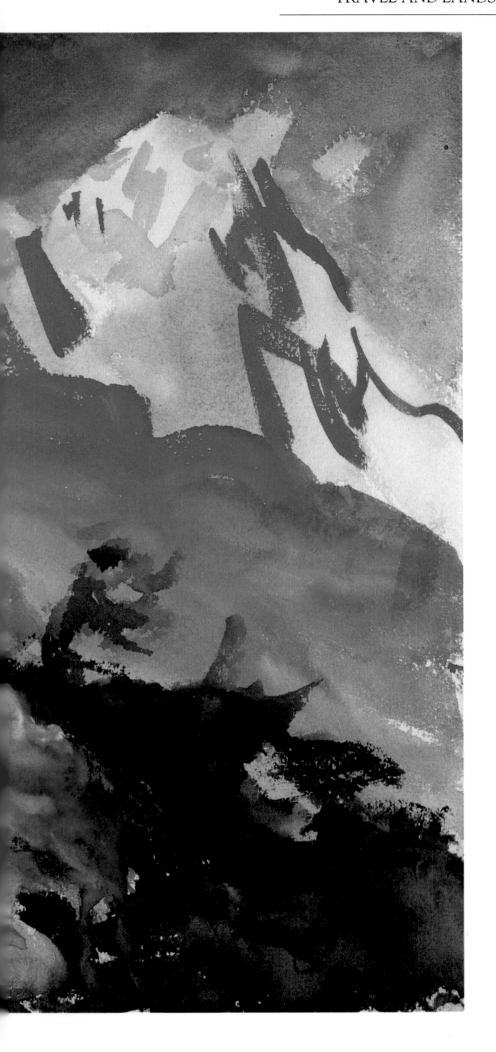

Mountain Fire
c. 1903-08, watercolor, 14×20 in.
Purchased by special subscription,
The Brooklyn Museum, NY
(09.831)

91

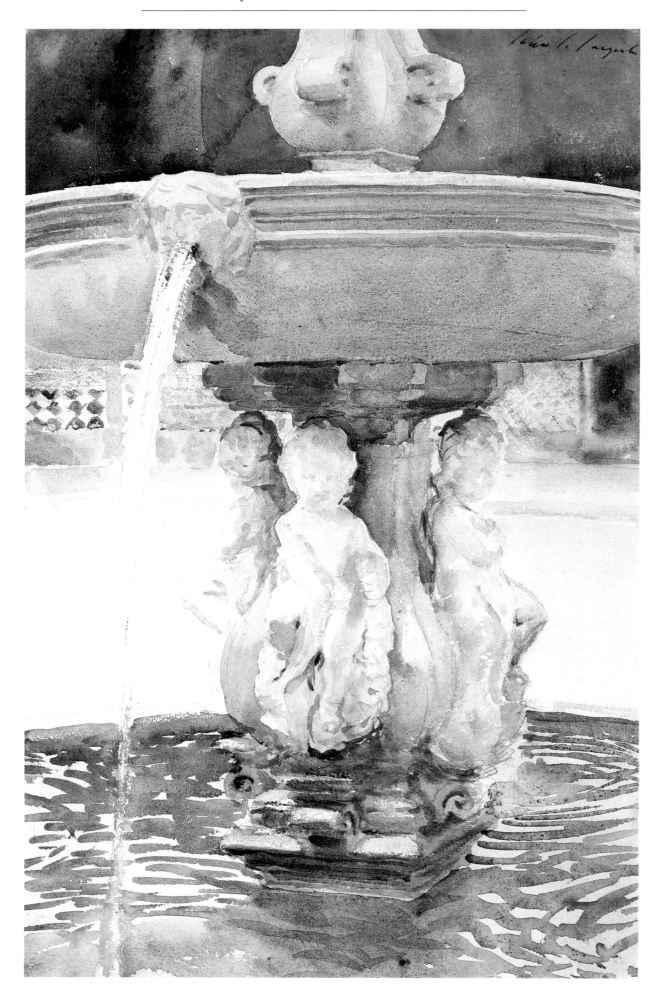

Spanish Fountain
c. 1914, watercolor and pencil on paper, 20⅞×13⁹⁄₁₆ in.
Purchase, Joseph Pulitzer Bequest, 1915,
The Metropolitan Museum of Art, New York, NY
(15.142.6)

Right:
Tiepolo Ceiling, Milan
c. 1904, watercolor on paper, 14×10 in.
Gift of Mrs. Francis Ormond, 1950,
The Metropolitan Museum of Art, New York, NY
(50.130.25)

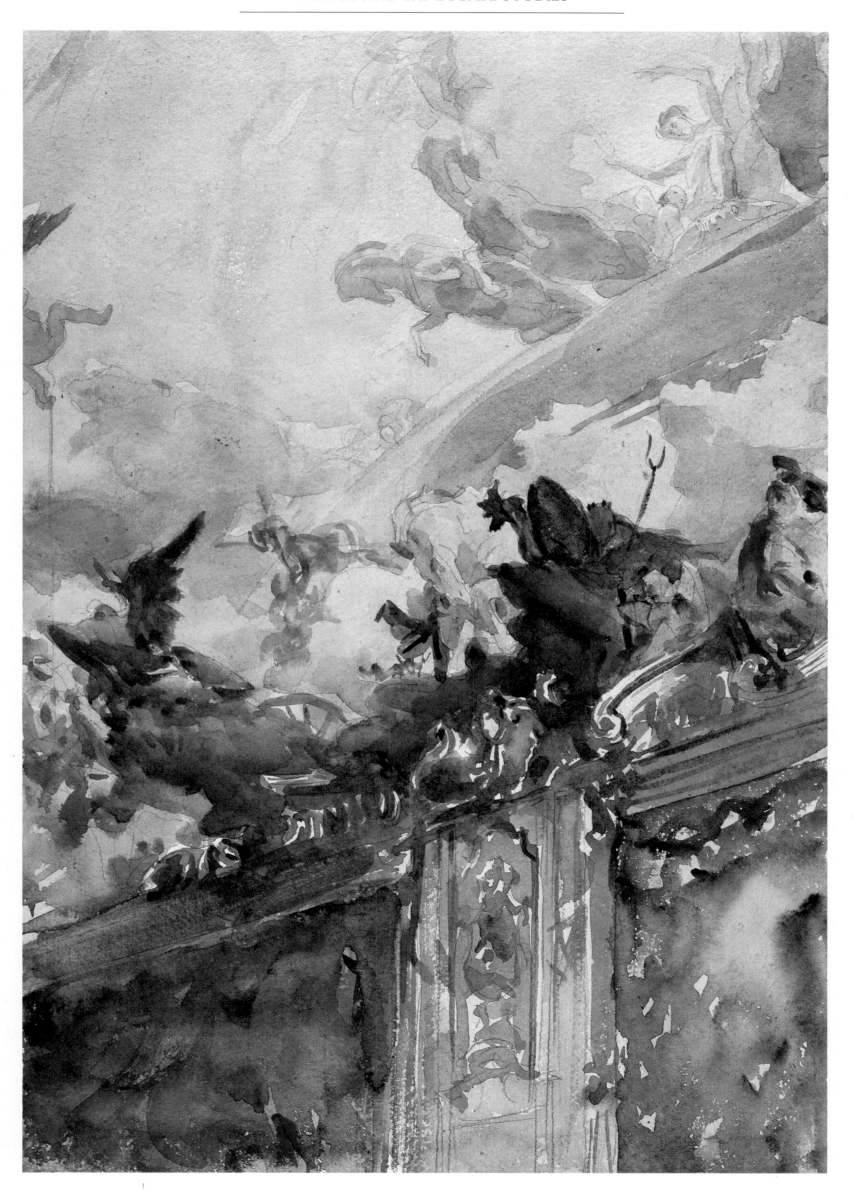

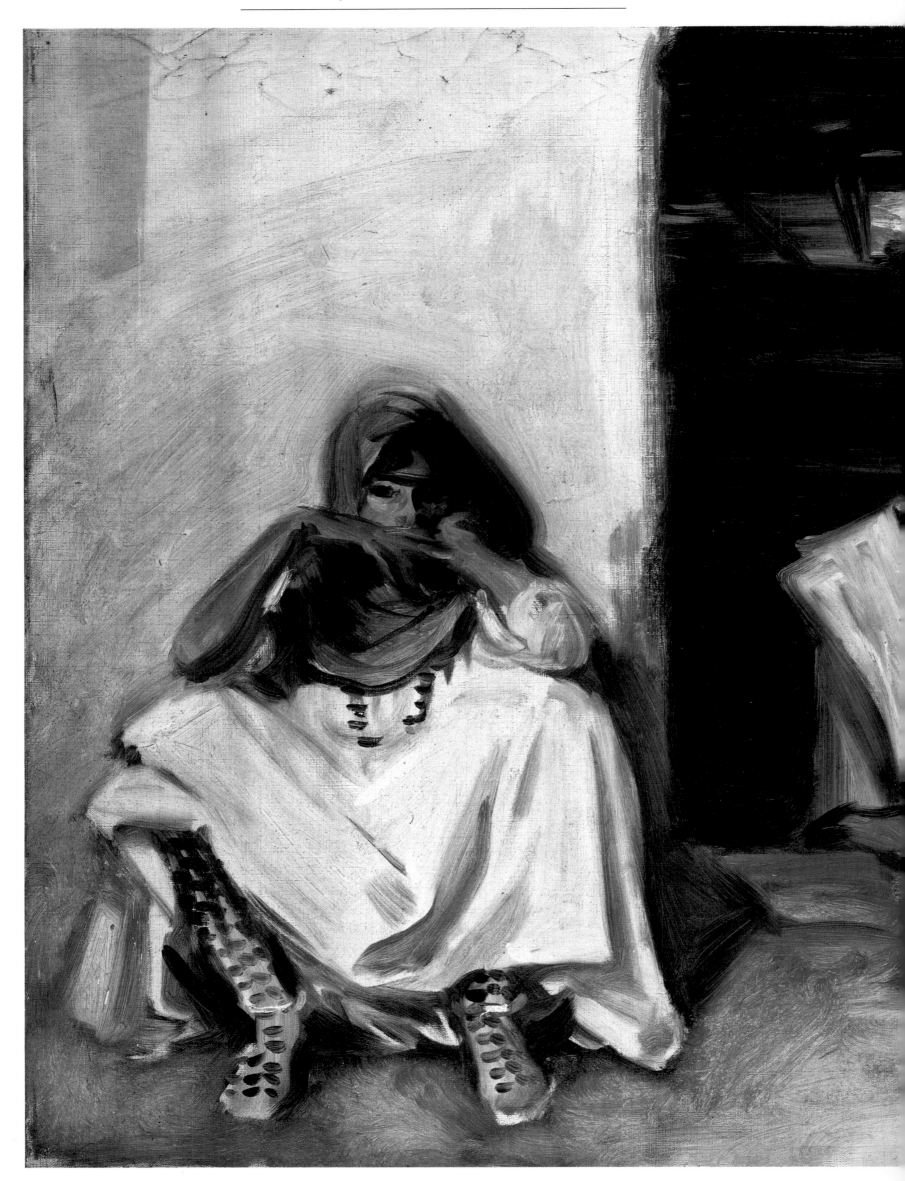

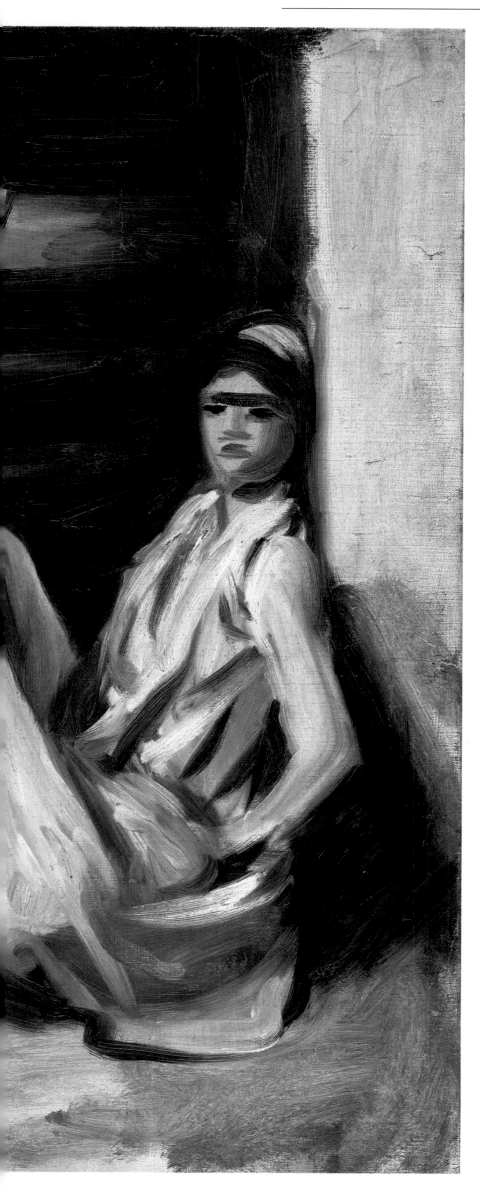

Two Arab Women
c. 1905, oil on canvas, 21×25¼ in.
Gift of Mrs. Francis Ormond, 1950,
The Metropolitan Museum of Art, New York, NY
(50.130.19)

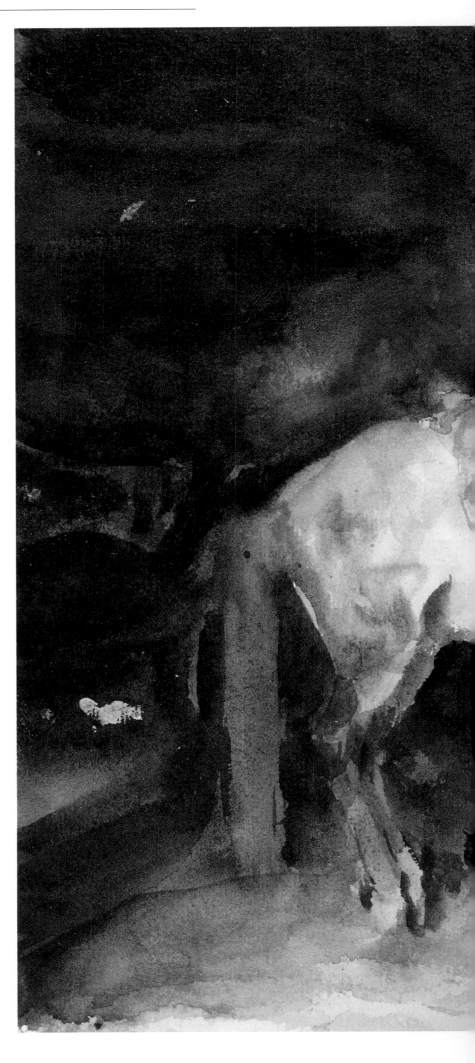

Arab Stable
1905-06, watercolor on paper, 10⅞×14⅜ in.
Special subscription fund,
The Brooklyn Museum, NY
(09.808)

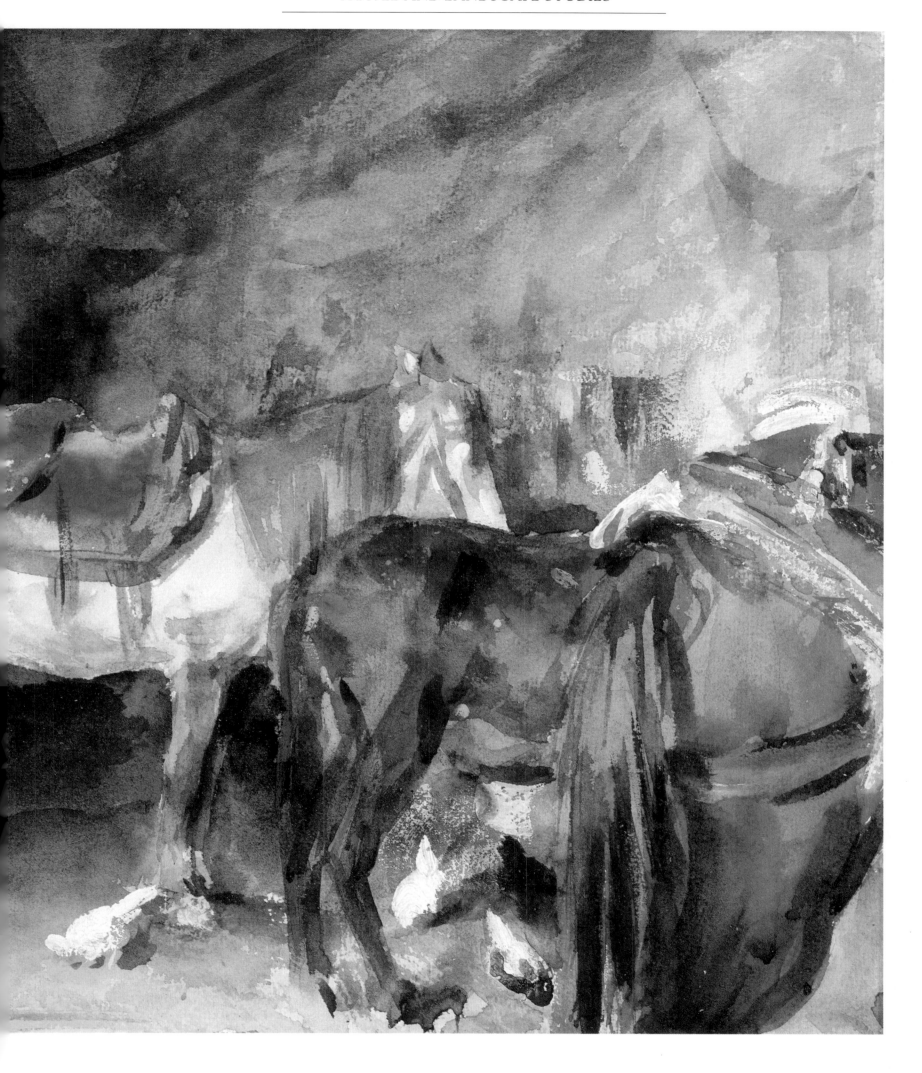

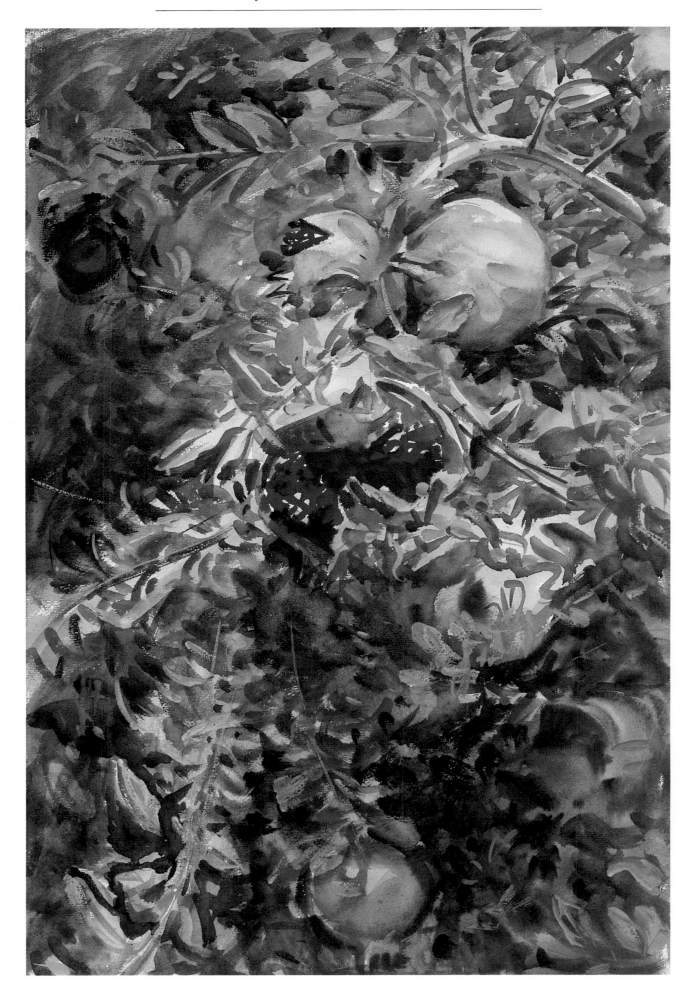

Pomegranates
1908, watercolor and pencil, 21³⁄₁₆×14⁷⁄₁₆ in.
Purchased by special subscription,
The Brooklyn Museum, NY
(09.832)

Right:
In a Medici Villa
c. 1907, watercolor and pencil, 12³⁄₁₆×14³⁄₈ in.
Purchased by special subscription,
The Brooklyn Museum, NY
(09.826)

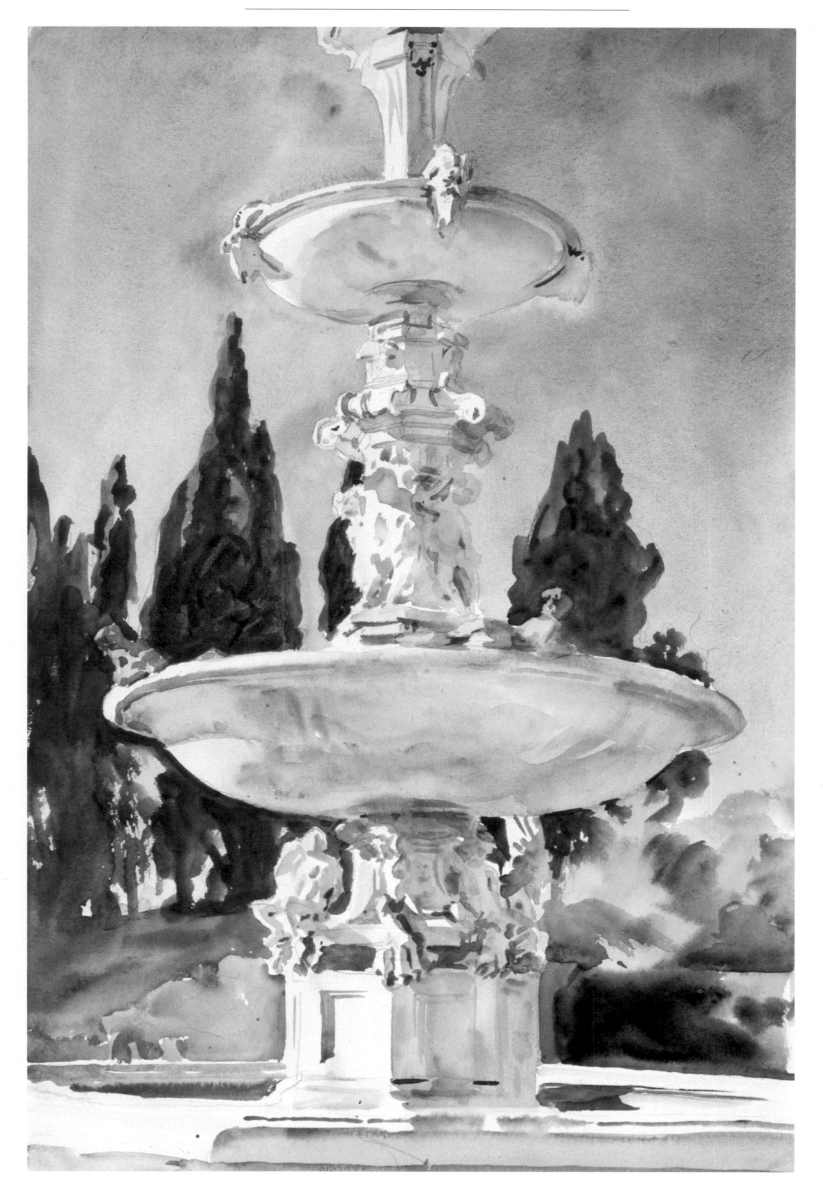

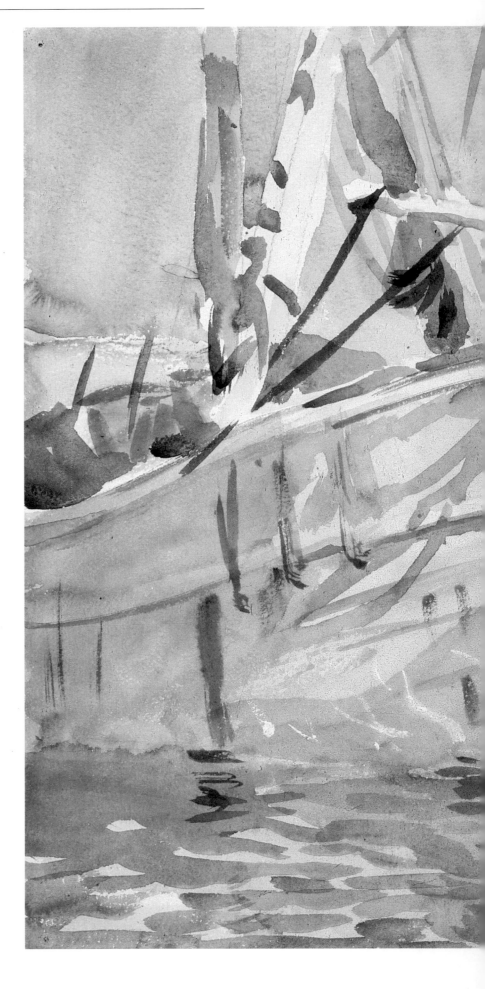

In a Levantine Port
c. 1905-06, watercolor and pencil, 12¹⁄₁₆×18⅛ in.
Purchased by special subscription,
The Brooklyn Museum, NY
(09.825)

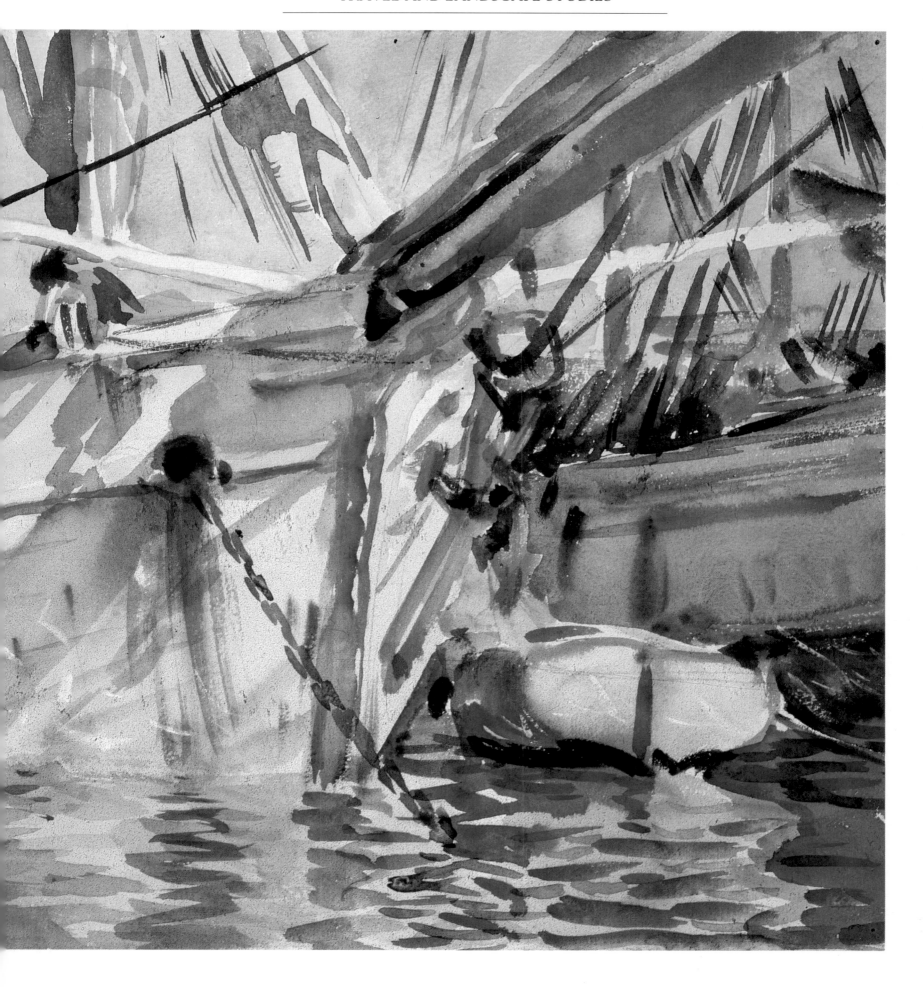

Overleaf:
Glacier Streams – The Simplon
c. 1910, oil in canvas, 34⅝×44¾ in.
The Horace P. Wright Collection,
Museum of Fine Arts, Springfield, MA

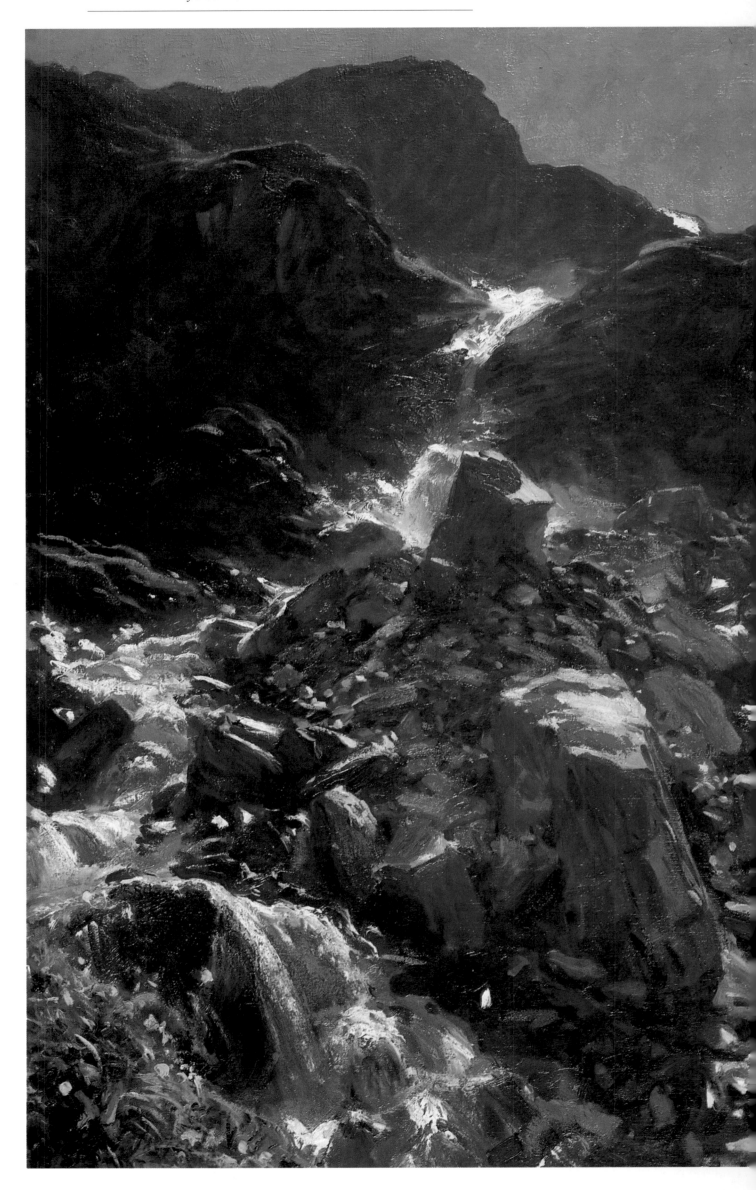

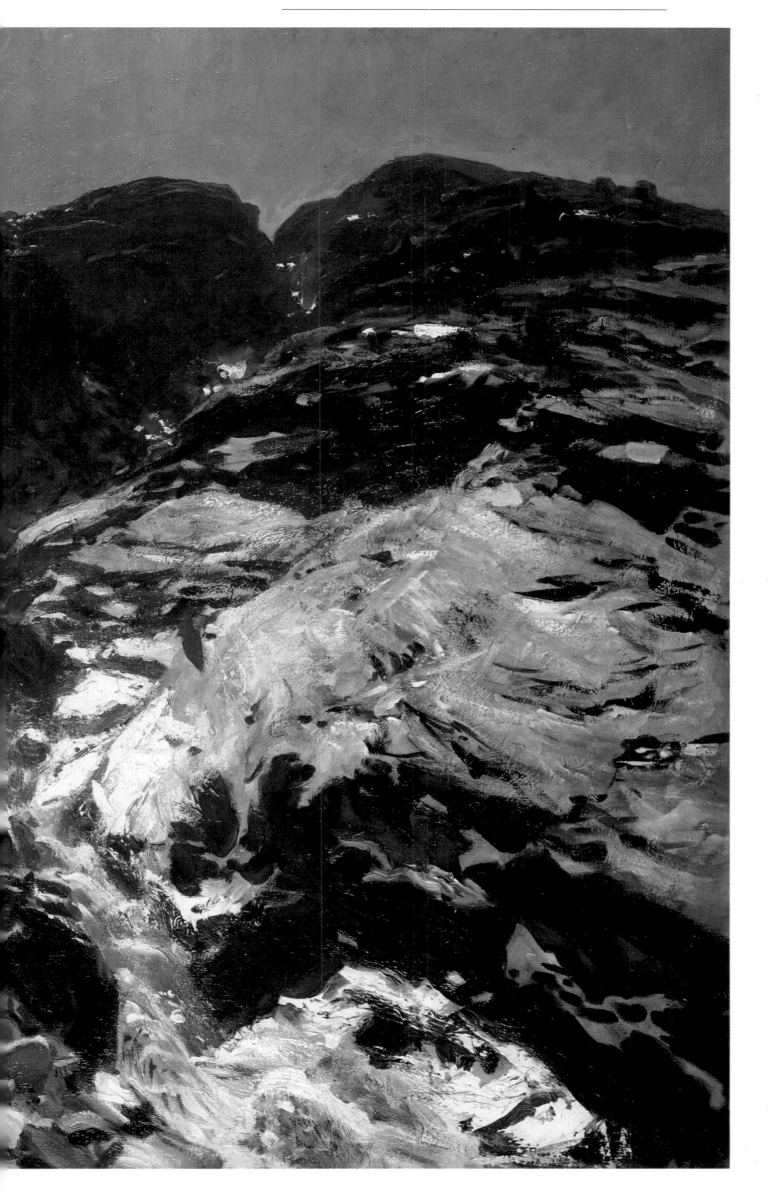

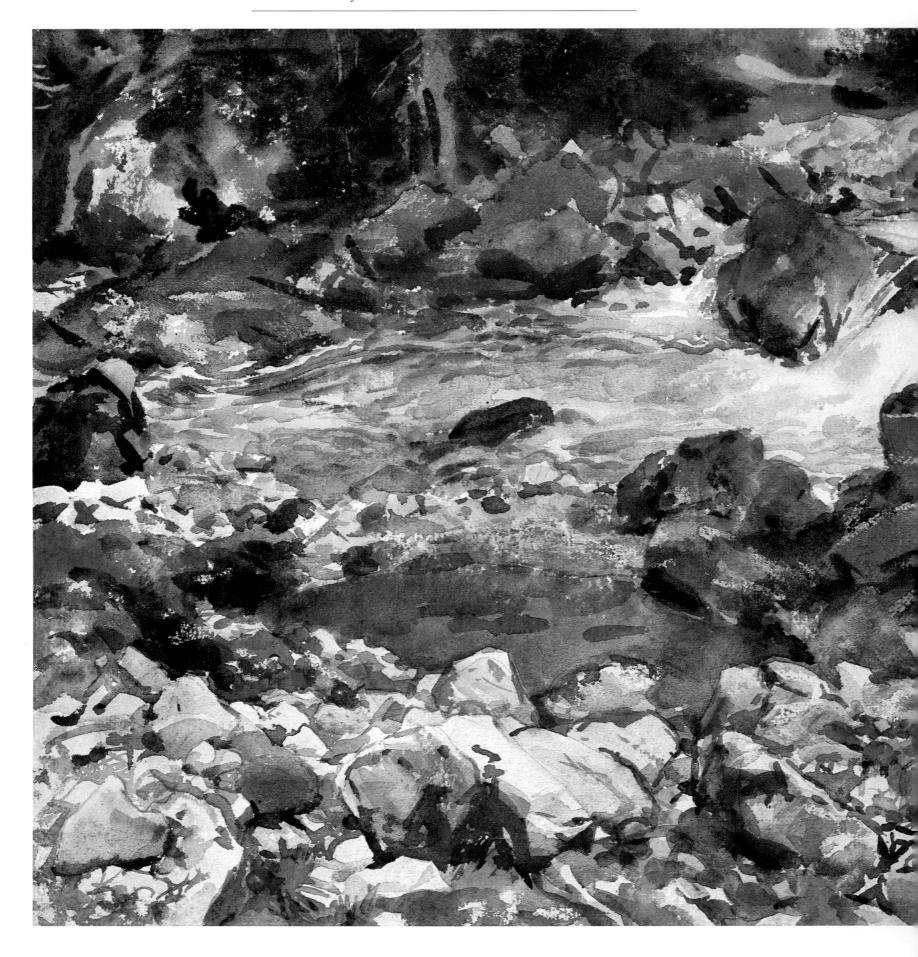

Mountain Stream
c. 1910-12, watercolor on paper, 13½×21 in.
Purchase, Joseph Pulitzer Bequest, 1915,
The Metropolitan Museum of Art, New York, NY
(15.142.2)

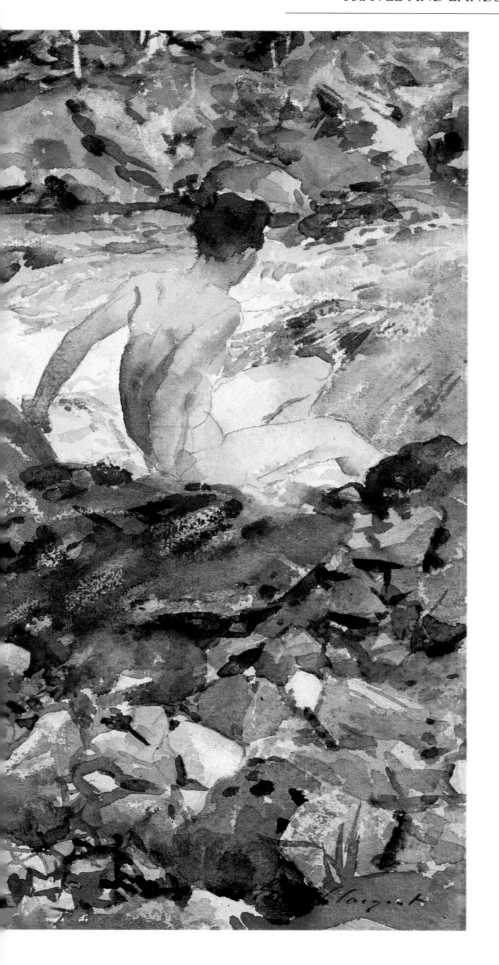

Overleaf:
In the Generalife
1912, watercolor on paper, 14¾×17⅞ in.
Purchase, Joseph Pulitzer Bequest, 1915,
The Metropolitan Museum of Art, New York, NY
(15.142.8)

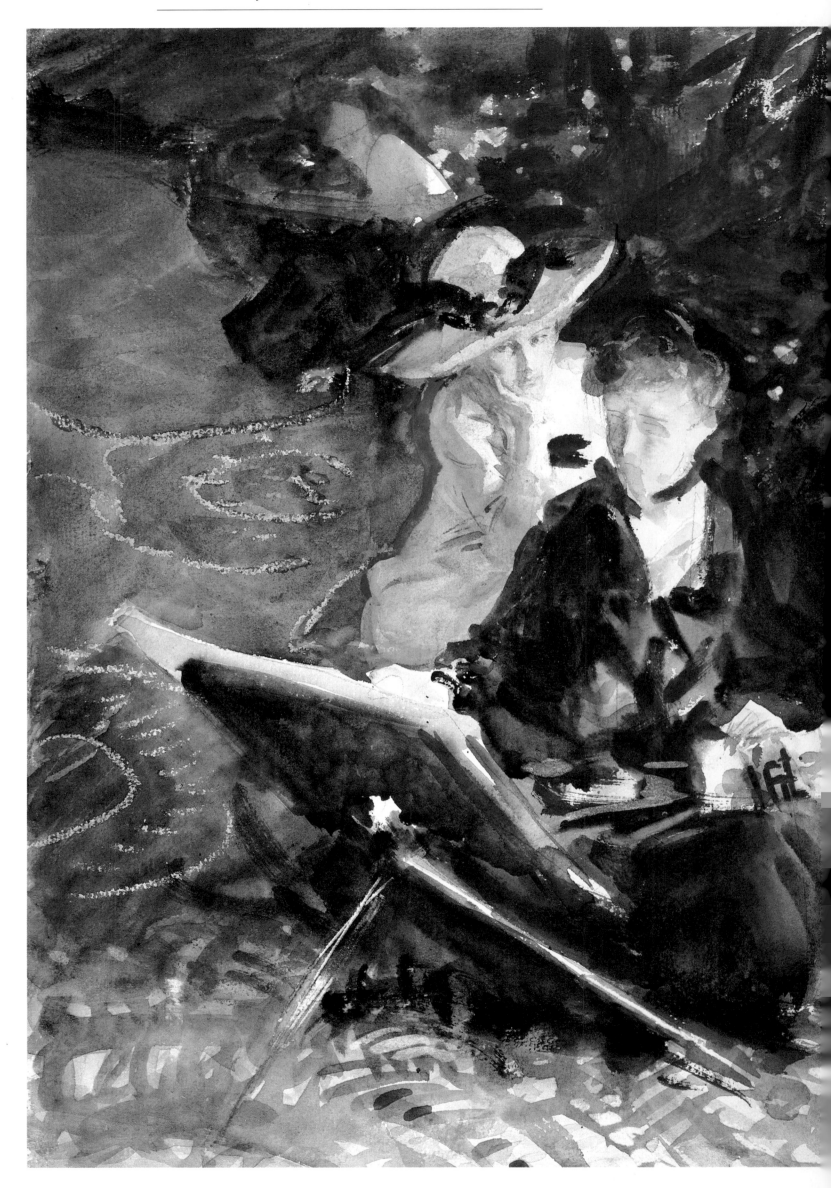

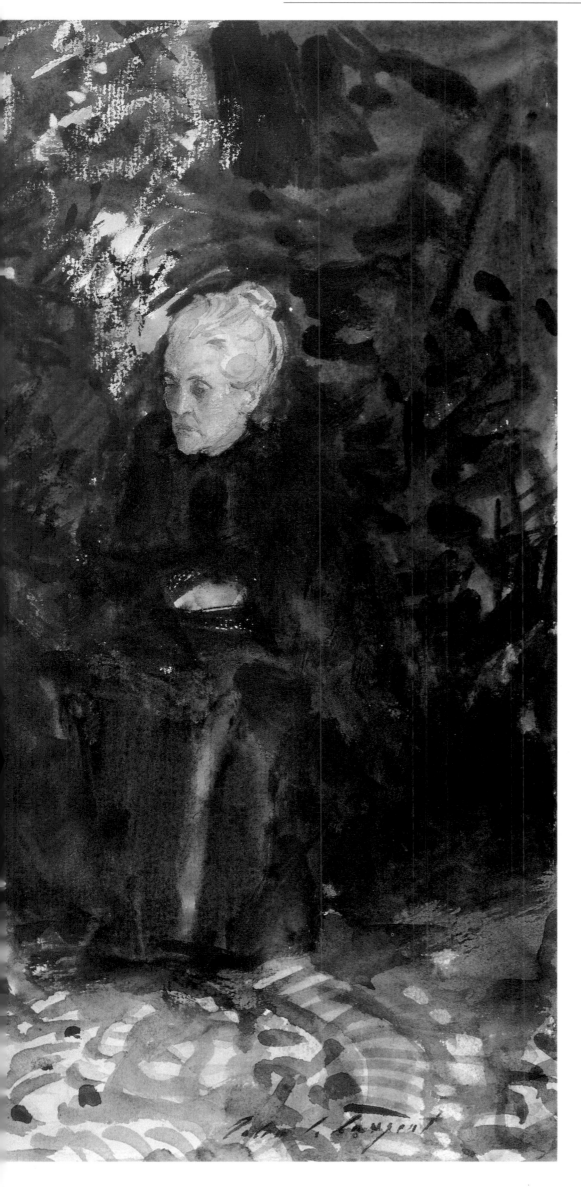

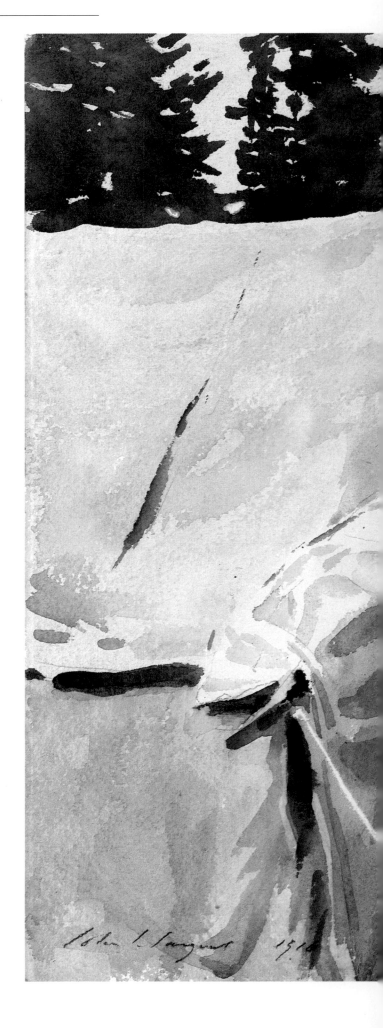

Camp at Lake O'Hara
1916, watercolor on paper, 15¾×21 in.
Gift of Mrs. David Hecht, in memory of her son
Victor D. Hecht, 1932,
The Metropolitan Museum of Art, New York, NY
(32.116)

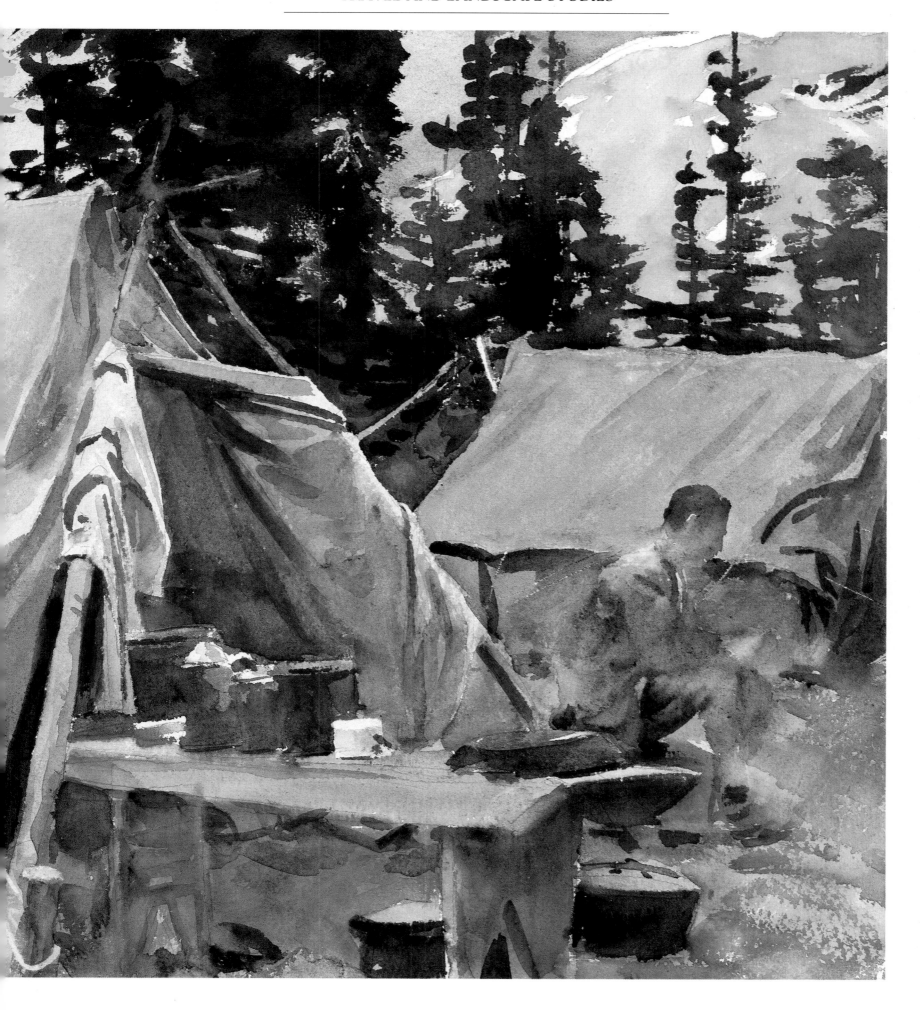

Overleaf:
Bringing Down Marble from the Quarries to Carrara
1911, oil on canvas, 28⅛×36⅛ in.
Harris Brisbane Dick Fund, 1917,
The Metropolitan Museum of Art, New York, NY
(17.97.1)

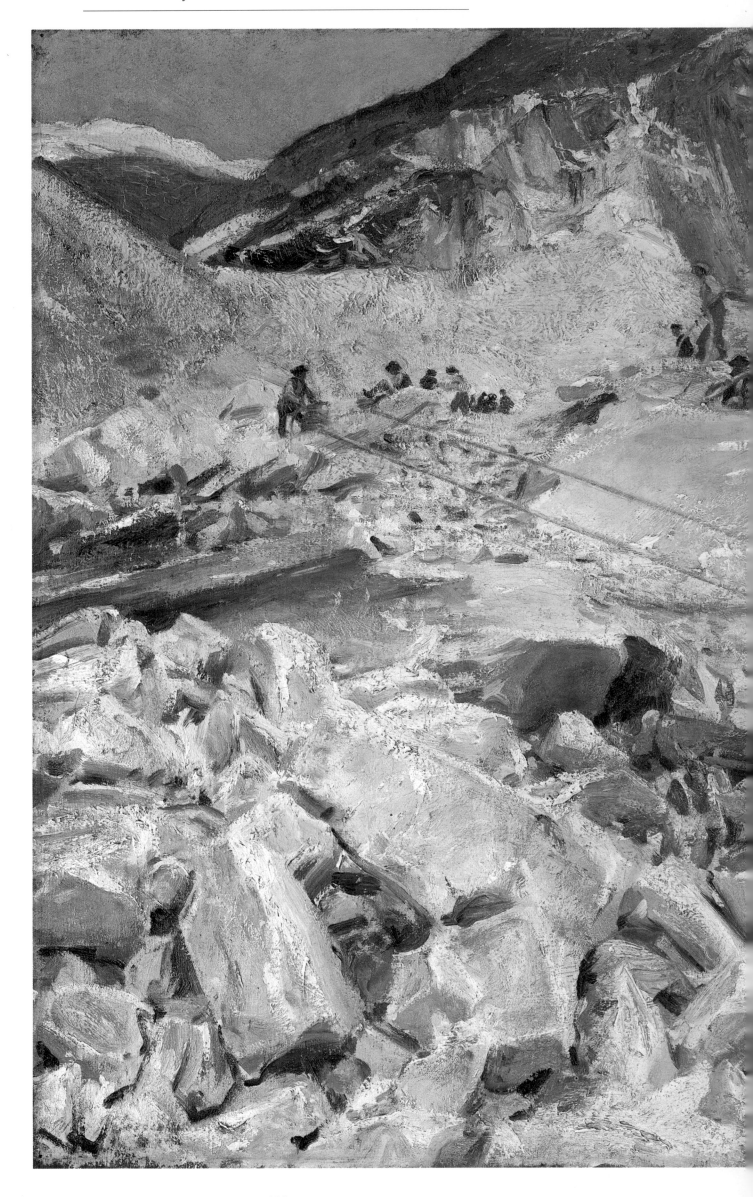